The Future of Being Human

BOOKS BY PAUL OLSEN

The Virgin of San Gil
Country of Old Men
Shadow of Me

THE
FUTURE
OF
BY PAUL OLSEN

BEING
HUMAN

 M. Evans and Company, Inc.
New York, N.Y. 10017

M. Evans and Company titles are distributed in
the United States by the J. B. Lippincott Company,
East Washington Square, Philadelphia, Pa. 19105;
and in Canada by McClelland & Stewart Ltd.,
25 Hollinger Road, Toronto M4B 3G2, Ontario

Library of Congress Cataloging in Publication Data

Olsen, Paul.
  The future of being human.
  Includes bibliographical references.
    1. Interpersonal relations. 2. Self-Actualization (Psychology)
3. Identity (Psychology) 4. United States—Social conditions—
1945-   I. Title.
HM132.O47   301.11   74-31004
ISBN 0-87131-173-9

Design by Madelaine Caldiero
Manufactured in the United States of America
9 8 7 6 5 4 3 2 1

For Vivian—Our Generation
And for Marissa and Matthew—Theirs

We shall assume that everyone is much more simply human than otherwise. . . .

HARRY STACK SULLIVAN

Contents

Acknowledgments

The ideas in this book were generated not by theory but by people, particularly by those very special people who come to my office, share their lives with me,, and thereby contribute to my humanness.

I owe a great many debts to a great many others, some of whom, if I named them all, might be perplexed if I cited them as influential in my thinking. Because many would disagree profoundly with what follows.

My deepest thanks to Dr. Kenneth Frank for his enduring friendship; to Jonathan Weiss for his much-needed loyalty; to Dr. Saul D. Miller for his unspoiled wisdom; to Dr. Roger A. MacKinnon whose clinical brilliance has been a constant source of excitement and developing knowledge; to Dr. Jerome Kosseff who once suggested that I bring my novelistic and clinical interests together in a book; to my colleagues at the National Institute for the Psychotherapies; and to Herbert M. Katz who did so much to bring these pages into being.

And to four people whom I have never met but whose impact upon my life has been incalculable: D. T. Suzuki, Ludwig Binswanger, Konrad Lorenz, and Michael Polanyi.

A final note: The anonymity of the people used in the illustrative material scattered throughout this book has been meticulously preserved. I doubt if they would recognize themselves; it is the essence that matters, not description.

1
The Struggle
to Be Human

The possession of people by people almost burned out an entire generation—mine. And now we are the ruling class, we who are in our forties.

We are the economic and intellectual architects of a badly crippled society in which the worth of a human being is measured largely by what he owns or by how desperately others covet what he has. We seem to know the price of everything but the value of almost nothing.

We also control the media—advertising, movies, publishing— and we are the backbone of psychiatry and the public relations industry. We don't *have* to be at the summit of political power, because we have the money, and we can influence more people to carry out our secret designs and desires than any other group in the history of mankind. The young people—our children— think they are free, but to a great extent we still control them. They are acting out the freedom that we wish for ourselves but cannot seize directly. We urge it covertly, yet on the surface recoil from it. And by and large we are only dimly aware of what we are really doing.

I came to this idea, which I will explore as fully as possible, from two directions—as a writer of fiction and as a psychotherapist. The work is different, but somewhere inside they meet and open into a system of personal realities, the most important one being that each direction I took was an attempt, a struggle, to find my humanity, to *become* a human being. Yet only when I became a therapist, engaged in my own therapy, did I *consciously* understand that what I could not do myself I had my fictional characters do for me. And now I suspect, in some cases *know*, that a therapist can do the same: he can help others to do things that he himself would not dare.

And so do we all—for good or ill. It is an oblique, sometimes bizarre, way of trying to discover our humanness. Because in a profound sense we do not yet know *how* to be human, and the search is elusive, painful, perplexing; the means to the end are largely unmapped except in the genetic code.

As I write this I am closing in on forty-two. In many ways it is a special age, sandwiched between two other generations, allowing a hard look at what the one ahead had us do for them and at what we had the one behind do for us. Jung liked to think that the forties are a time of mellowness, of acceptance and fuller insight into the purpose of life. But that is too vague, even too mystical. The value of this age is in that forward and backward and present perspective, and the question is not *what is the meaning of life?* but *how closer have we come to being more human?*—and why is the goal so agonizingly difficult when other animals have no need of the question at all?

When I began to understand that I lived my life, as most of us do, in episodes instead of continuity, in minor triumphs and tragedies, still another realization took root. Not one of those fabled transcendental explosions of insight, but something that quietly surfaced from within me where it had been all the while, awaiting discovery. I began to see that my odyssey of over forty years, my struggle to find myself, was no more, no less, than struggling to become a human being. The search for identity and the search for humanness are not just inseparable. They are identical.

Since the concept of *individual* is so precious to our species, ingrained actually, the search must begin on a personal level. And since it is necessarily "selfish," it usually dulls us to the great truth that what we are looking for is the fulfillment of our potentiality as a person. Once that is achieved, even closely approximated, then we become what we were meant to become. More than human is an impossibility, less than human a travesty. An infant attempts this fulfillment without even knowing that he tries; he follows the pattern of his genetic possibilities. But soon the pattern is distorted—and then the ease in becoming human is converted into a struggle.

I doubt if there is anyone on earth disengaged from this struggle, except that most of us are not aware of it—and that is why such a simple truth can be experienced as a powerful revelation. Yet it is essentially the only truth there is: *I am human.*

We live as if we are our own self-contained mystery stories, overlooking our clues, hopelessly puzzled by others, doing and becoming things we think we are clear about only to find ourselves confused, at sea, at times disenchanted and bitter, sometimes suicidal. We do not know how to be human because we do not know ourselves.

In trying to become human a person takes a beating. Suffering should not be necessary to become human, yet we have come to believe that suffering *is* the human condition. To some extent it still is, and in desperation we have turned it into a virtue.

To refocus my own life as an attempt to be human is to refocus much of what I have felt, thought, and done as components of the struggle. I must also be aware of the ways in which I have been dehumanized—not by Nazis or madmen, but by people who hadn't a glimmer of awareness that they were engaged in a dehumanizing process. I must look and use what I see, in a balanced way, without self-glorification or a need for revenge: otherwise I dehumanize myself.

If you refocus it this way, I think that anyone's life is clearer. Clearer, not simpler. Then a life is no longer a matter of achieving glory, power, wealth, attunement to nature, even earning a living wage. A life, then, becomes a process aimed at achieving the status of human being. The means may be totally cockeyed, distorted, illusory—but they *are* aimed at the general direction of the target.

The struggle, too, needs a shift in focus: better put, it is a struggle to reestablish, regain, feelings and connectedness with others and with the sense of being alive. Most, if not all, of us were raped of something naturally human—and the struggle resides precisely in getting back what we were born with, what belongs to us, what we have the right to call our own. This restoration is the core of psychotherapy—and psychotherapy is the arena where the struggle is *consciously* entered, where it is recognized and identified.

Society seems to command that we all be reared by having our humanness pinched off in one way or another. And yet there is always that gnawing truth that society is our own creation. The only way out of the paradox is that we are many societies, with the one in power having gotten there by arousing a variety of needs and welding them into a majority—the majority then falling to pieces because it was an illusion in the first place. (For example, in 1960 I might have voted for Kennedy for any, or any combination of, the following reasons: belief in promised reform; his attractiveness and class; a dislike or distrust of Nixon; sympathy with Catholicism, etc. *All* these factors assured his victory—not a single-minded unity.) Thus attitudes rarely budge and we remain parochial. But important here is the easily observable fact that humanistically oriented societies are notoriously short-lived. In small countries they are quickly obliterated, usually by army officers. In large countries humanism is subverted from the top, the power structure: a real or illusory external enemy is created, or the economy threatens to fail. And then we close up, abandon those qualities which are unique to humans, and fall back on what is common to any animal: we become afraid of attack, establish pecking orders, get preoccupied with basic survival. We cannot hold fast to our humanness: fear of attack precludes even kindness. If we are kept in fear, we can be controlled by an incredibly small number of people who play the game of power.

Without this periodic return to dehumanization there would be no novelists attempting to restore human values, no psycho-therapists searching for human music in purely animal noise, no concepts of freedom, no revolutions. There would be very little need for the struggle. And I don't mean utopianism, which is ideology. But I can safely say that if *all* people achieved full humanness—well, we haven't the foggiest idea what that would mean in terms of what we could become.

As it stands, you try it your own way, and I tried it first through fiction—at least formally, though every experience of my life led to that point. Consequently my writing has never been purely entertainment, but always a reflection of a grasp at a partially lost sense of myself. (My generation can laugh at times, but it is almost monumentally serious.) But ultimately writing was not enough—not enough because it is mainly vicarious and the act itself takes place in isolation and detachment from others. Nothing there but my thoughts, fantasies, and a one-way com-munication to an invisible audience—which is really talking to yourself. Working with my characters, their conflicts and wishes and hopes, was very much like being a voyeur peeping at my own humanity.

That, of course, is retrospect: I could not have said it then because I knew it only on an intuitive level, articulated in the heart, not the head. Later on there was an even more startling piece of knowledge, startling because it was immediately surprising, then just as immediately it was no surprise at all. I became a psychotherapist not only to make contact with others, to learn and help, but the becoming led logically into my own therapy, into my own process of rediscovery and restoration.

I have known a number of therapists who came to the same conclusion, then promptly submerged into depressions. They were also searching for their humanity but they simply did not want to believe that becoming a therapist was an oblique route, a roundabout way of knocking at the door. It disturbed them to discover that just beneath the desire to help others was the powerful wish to help themselves. The professional goal was tainted; their whole way of life suddenly seemed "neurotic," out of control, spooky, sick. Yet the logic of it all was perfect: helping others and helping oneself is completely reciprocal. Which is why the best psychotherapists of any theoretical orientation permit themselves to be reminded of their humanity by their patients, permit their patients to *contribute* to their humanity, to expand and enrich it. Indeed, this is exactly what patients emotionally insist upon: that their therapists be human beings. It sort of keeps you honest—if you are at all inclined that way. And it is no more than a friend would ask—or a child of a parent.

I have always been aware of the dehumanizing process, but by dehumanization I don't mean cold technological control or the pollution of the air and rivers. Once rivers were pristine, yet we still had trouble locating our humanity. Theologians and philosophers tried to explain it all and the effort led to centuries of a belief that life was suffering, misery. What I mean by dehumanization is the loss of knowledge about ourselves, the murder of our feelings, the avoidance of searching within—which results in a propensity for vicarious living. We simply do not experience most of what we are all about, and this is why the search for our humanity is so difficult a struggle. We emphasize every possible external means of explaining our "purpose," making us happy, giving us stature. But we turn away from the one thing, really the only thing, that differentiates us from all other animals—the majestic complexity of our inner lives. Dealing with this complexity should logically precede explorations of the moon, of Mars, but we do not act logically. Perhaps we never have. Quite likely we must face an incredible possibility: that running off to outer space is a flamboyant way of running away from ourselves. Because what does the feather of the moon, stuck in our caps, do to aid the emergence of our humanness? Moon travel is something we are capable of because we are clever. The Wright brothers were clever and so was the person who discovered the wheel, but these "achievements" do not reveal *conscious* insight about being human. They only reflect one aspect of ourselves: intelligence. We know that brain-damaged people score low on IQ tests; but they can be intensely human, their struggle to *be* human no less dynamic than the majority of us blessed with adequate intellectual equipment.

Scientists will tell us that an exploration of the moon may reveal more data about our origins—or at least the origins of our planet. Whether this data reveals anything of our inner life remains to be seen; I suspect that it won't.

This will not be a doomsday book. Doomsday books are written by people who do not realize the human potentiality inherent in what we do not know of ourselves—a whole inner life bubbling toward conscious expression, emerging so often in strange, seemingly inexplicable ways. Prophets of the death of our species consistently fail to perceive a crucial fact: *we are all struggling to be human, and nothing more.* And in the struggle there is hope, not to achieve miracles, but to become, at last, full members of a human community.

2
Out There, the Wall

Much of my life has been aimed at getting loose, de-possessing myself, feeling what is mine to feel—distinguishing what I am from what I was supposed to be. To me, that is the heart of the struggle to be human, anyone's struggle.

Like all generations, mine has had particular problems in trying to locate its human core; and like all generations, it has a unique personality which expresses itself in its influence upon its children and upon society as a whole. What I mean is this: you can observe a generation, even study it sociologically, and arrive at a list of traits and attitudes common to most of its members. What you are then describing is merely behavior—perhaps a catalog of behaviors, of *observable* data. But the essence of what a generation is all about lies beneath the surface: it lies in the multitude of hidden wishes and urges that are rarely, if ever, acted upon. We are able to identify them really in only one way —by coming to the conclusion that these covert wishes are expressed for us by our children and hence by the entire generation behind us. We have wielded the incredible power of parenthood to make of our children what we are so afraid to be.

It is important to reemphasize that those of us in our forties are now the ruling class, climbing steadily toward greater positions of influence and power, already the directors of mass media, the spine of the middle class. We have enormous social clout. At the same time we are self-absorbed, wary of others, a bit terrified by the unknown, unsettled by change. Our generational world view is agonizingly ambivalent; we want to recapture the missing links of our youth by living through our children, yet we are often repelled and horrified by what we have gotten them to do for us. Because—except for moments of extreme crisis or exceptional emotional honesty—we are not aware of what *we* are doing.

A remarkable event led to the unique social context in which much of my generation was reared. I believe that what happened to us was very much the end product of our parents' response to a world turned suddenly upside down, a world turned brutal, a world in which people were defeated, sapped, and rendered impotent. Not the frustrated helplessness of a grinding war, public or secret, somewhere far off in Asia, but an event that exploded the dreams of everyday soup-in-the-pot life. It was the Depression, and with it came the destruction of any sense that a person had even the smallest voice in his personal destiny.

Promised everything by a paper economy and fraudulent guarantees of security, floating euphorically along on a postwar national image of invulnerability and of having saved the world from what, that year, the world needed saving from, there was, suddenly, *nothing*. That everyone was making it in the twenties was actually pure myth; but everyone was supposed to make it, was almost obligated to. From the indoctrinated point of view of the little man, all you had to do was trade paper for paper, sit back, watch a few columns of numbers, and in a fortnight you would be drinking champagne by the magnum. Naturally it was the ordinary people who were devastated; they had little to begin with, and less for them was nothing at all.

We children were all our parents, the little people, had left, and they clutched us desperately. They grew to possess us with the fanaticism of misers rubbing fingertips over gold coin. It had to be. Probably, it had to be. And it was shatteringly predictive of things to come.

In the jargon of the social sciences, and particularly of psychoanalysis whose popularity rose as the stock market declined toward World War II, our parents overprotected us, fostered our dependence upon them. But the jargon canot remotely convey the sense of how completely they possessed us or the impact of their ownership. We were to them what the huge gaudy automobile was, perhaps still is, to many Negroes—the single important symbol owned as a substitute for a decent home, a steady job, and ultimately as a substitute for a self. We were definitively owned, we belonged to them, and we were branded, imprinted, with their view of the world: it was base, attacking, terrifying, depriving, peopled by an alien Them who lived Out There beyond the walls. (We might have liked each other if we hadn't all been Them Out There to each other.) It was largely a paranoid vision, and it contributed to our awe of force and power, our fear of social protest, our feeling of terrible vulnerability whenever we ventured into the outer world of vicious strangers. Our parents protected us from this world, and as we grew we relied more and more upon their protection, finally adopting their view as our own. It is a view of the world from which we have never recovered.

Reflection: If there was a hero, soon to become the antihero, a concept that my generation has commercialized as it does almost everything it simultaneously wishes to be and feels anxiety about, a man who epitomized the frustration and impotence of all of us, it was Pete Reiser, the *Wünderkind* outfielder of the Brooklyn Dodgers. In 1942 he was destined to become perhaps the greatest baseball player in the history of the game, and for many of us he was already incomparable. Ted Williams, the

"Splendid Splinter" of the other league, was no more than the stick on a Good Humor. Pete Reiser was "The Pistol." And he could do it all—run, field, throw, but especially hit—with an authority that caught your breath short. Crackling line drives, making you convinced that bat and ball *had* to feel pain.

In the pennant drive of 1942, with Reiser nearing .400 and getting stronger, it happened: chasing a long fly he crashed into the outfield wall and crumpled. No Reiser, no pennant. And it was to happen again and again. After the war years, in 1946, although he was still fast and stole home enough times to set a record, he was done, he could not really face a ball speeding toward him at 100 miles per hour. If you looked closely and remembered what he had been, you saw a shell—a fast shell who stole what he could no longer demand with his bat. In that year of 1946 he began capriciously to fool with switch-hitting—the mark of a confused man with a moribund self-confidence, searching for magic.

And then he was gone, and his legacy was proof that you had to be wary, that to give everything fully and recklessly was to court disaster. The wall out there, the wall against which he repeatedly broke his talent as if possessed by an evil demon, was our wall too. It was the Out There that we were raised to fear. He challenged it and lost, continued to lose until he was, or seemed, addled. The wall won and we could never again watch an outfielder tear hellbent after a fly ball without feeling a bolt of panic, even terror.

Yet we identified with Pete Reiser because we also felt special. Kept from the outside world, we were nurtured on fantasies of our importance without a thought of weaning. We were the center of the family, more important than a wife or husband, the future hope, the living wish geared to fulfill all that our parents could not accomplish, to regain what they had lost. And within our tiny gray worlds we were insufferable children—spoiled, egotistic, delicate, easily hurt and shamed—and when we were sent into the streets and schools we suffered the torments of the damned.

We quivered in the presence of the "tough" kids, the bullies, and there were plenty of them. But they would (little consolation) grow up to be truck drivers, ditchdiggers, and busboys while we would use our brains to build the new middle class. They could shatter us simply by doubling a fist at us from a block away. We were already like ancient Oriental pottery webbed with fine cracks, but we had a far lower tensile strength. We ran from confrontations and turned paralytic at the mere hint of a fight. In my neighborhood the tough kids liked to form a circle around us, then demand that we show our penises—and the sweat of terror would cascade because we were not sure that we could find them.

As I've sharply underlined, we came to consider almost everyone as a member of Out There—in a position of personal, individualized intimidation. But there existed a real Out There that we—Jews, Catholics, any other minority group—would not come to see clearly until we grew up, namely, the social power structure, perpetuated by the people we eventually called WASPs. And I don't mean Protestantism as a loosely defined religious concept. I mean *power*. This structure was what we ultimately had to crash; on conscious or unconscious levels it was the model for our parents' aspirations even though many of our fathers unionized against it, fought it, railed at it with impotent curses.

At first glance it might seem ridiculous that my contemporaries, Protestants entrenched in this power structure, had to wrestle with an Out There. Weren't *they* the Out There? How could the enviable envy, the powerful cringe?

Yet they did, then *as* now, but in a very different way. For them, Out There is the family itself—the parents, all the older members. While what *I* call and identify with as *we* were the precious possessions of our parents, their potential saviors and status-raisers, Protestant children must earn a place in the family structure itself, proving that they are worthy of the inheritance.

In emotional terms this is a desperate situation for a child; the pain is incredible.

Patients from this background are, to me, plainly frightening. What appears to be snobbery, conformity, haughtiness, forms the patina upon an emotional coldness that makes human relatedness a crippled thing. Relatedness for these people is established via manners, morals, trivial social rules, and profoundly repressed hostility which emerges as sarcasm, hauteur, and veiled competitiveness. These are the children who must be seen and not heard. Literally.

These people have been possessed by their parents along different lines. Not by smothering, humoring, unrealistic fantasies, but by withdrawal and distance and cold criticism, by requiring that the child constantly seek parental acceptance. The child is never quite *in* the family. By his status as child he is trivial, not truly a person, an object of constant appraisal who is rarely kissed or hugged. He must not show emotion since that alienates his parents. Yet rarely will he be slapped or yelled at: he will be rejected, abandoned, cut—*on premisis*. At the table, in the living room, anywhere. While many children fear being put out of the family, these people fear that they can never get in.

In their common fantasies and early memories they knock at the doors of houses without gaining admittance; they walk alone through empty rooms; they eat silent meals while looking vast distances *up* at their parents; in dreams some have talked with furniture and paintings. Often these memories and dreams are unpeopled. When people do appear they usually do not talk, but stare blanky or reproachfully. Later, when such people are absorbed into the power structure, ruthlessness is simple to execute, since no feeling has ever been appropriate in relating to others. I think that it is this way of being in the world that we have come to associate with Protestantism—not really a religious idea at all.

These patients often bolt therapy. They cannot tolerate the closeness of the relationship unless it develops with infinite slowness. By a stunning irony the therapist becomes a threat—an Out There whose plot is to touch emotion. Indeed, the chief complaint of these patients is remarkably similar: some emotion has escaped through their guard and they want it controlled. They want to be rid of it. And, like the parents of these people, the therapist is supposed to show them the way, to reteach them how to be "good."

Perhaps it is at least this that unites all the members of my generation: all of us got along mainly with adults since the vast majority of us were *good*. But my peers and I in the power structure were strangers in our goodness, our specialness, and so no one can really see much similarity between us: there are the old wealthy and the *nouveau riche*, the driver of the garish Cadillac and the unostentatious Shaker Heights millionaire in his eight-year-old, bashed-in Dodge. Those of the real Out There came to understand their specialness only later in life, when they were finally admitted into the family and its prestige. We knew it from the year one—in *our* common memories of being beamed at and gloated over by our parents.

We were pampered blind by illusory, almost delusional, airs and postures that masked the rotten salaries of our fathers (when they worked), the suppers of two-cent fish cakes, and the yammering of landlords. So precious were we that our mothers squeezed our blackheads lest we be flawed in even ordinary ways. And eventually we became con men of the highest order. What we got, we got by crying and whining and whimpering, and we were teachers' pets, performing dogs at the local freak show. Owned. Trained.

What our parents could not or did not want to know was that they were prepping us for major surgery without anesthesia. The world was sharpening its scalpel beyond the walls. Out There we would come to flee real conflict, to relate to others only in ways calculated to reduce fear and save face, to develop a repertory of security devices staggering in their inventiveness and variation. To preserve our identity as *objets d'art*, we dared not be touched. Possessed by our parents, we would in turn come to assume an entrepreneurial role in order to stock the depleted inventories of our hearts. Our lives, like the lives of our parents, would become vicarious—but in very different ways.

Perhaps the one emotion we had that gave us some sense of being alive was our anger, an anger that evolved really from two roots: frustration when, entitled to everything, we could not get something; and a reaction to our feelings of domination and entrapment. The latter, of course, is a more productive anger: it can be converted into *some* form of assertiveness and independence. But our anger was intolerable to our parents. It signified, as it still signifies, a certain spirit, a kind of protestation of self, and it seemed to have a life of its own, perhaps a vitality, that challenges ownership. It must be stifled; the toy must realize that it cannot crank up itself.

So, too, with our sexuality, certainly a strong sign of vitality: it was undermined, forbidden expression; our genitals were not our own to contemplate or use. So there is a musty, moribund quality to our personal engagement in sex. We can take it or leave it, mostly leave it, especially if it leads to intimate contact with another person and thus becomes a threat to our defensive self-involvement. But at a distance sex is fine. My generation is a voyeuristic one, because voyeurism is by definition a distance from others. If the houselights were suddenly raised at a showing of a pornographic film—which one of us no doubt produced— you would see the abashed, guilty, trapped faces of men in their forties and early fifties. It all remains as voyeuristic, passive, and masturbatory as it was in our adolescence.

As teen-agers we were mawkish and awkward, and we could not push through that anxiety-soaked inner prohibition that would have allowed us to form a true bond with others. It was an age of waiting, the boys for the girls, the girls for the boys, waiting for something to happen. Any move risked rejection, an intolerable humiliation and hurt. We waited for girls to let us kiss them while, in the dark of a movie balcony, hiding our erections, we necked with the backs of their seats, fingers creeping silently toward distant shoulders. On a local road that dissected a cemetery, we used to hunt for discarded condoms: apparently people really *did it*. *Girls* did it. The thought was nerve-splitting. But where were they, those girls who did it? No doubt in a VD hospital, catatonic, with black concave eye sockets and suppurating lips. Sex was totally cut off from love.

And we waited to be drafted. We waited out Joseph McCarthy —who hung himself with no one's help but his own. We waited out everything, but chose the right professions—yet waiting, too, for the spanking bright teams of businessmen who came to whisk us off campus into the adventure of the American economy. We waited because what we needed with the urgency of air to breathe was the preservation of our specialness and goodness, and we maintained them paradoxically through external conformity. Yet at second glance it was no paradox at all: for in buffering ourselves against the dangers of Out There we sought immunity, and there is no better road to immunity than via disappearance. My generation, lately called the Silent Majority, is not merely silent. Wielding its power, it is faceless, all but vanished in its internal drabness, but proud in the ownership of symbols—cars, homes, an infinity of appliances—doing its loyal best to drive up the prices of wine, real estate, anything that lends it status. All of these things are inherently no more than what they are. Things. It is the way we have come to use them that bares the essence of what we lack as human beings—meaning, knowledge, and, ultimately, *self*-possession.

We seem to be a generation bred on and surrounded by catastrophe, and still another near cataclysm fueled our pilgrimage toward ownership and conformity. World War II reversed the

Depression and unfurled the banners proclaiming affluence. Our parents were jubilant; most still had enough juice left to work in war plants. But their decade-long vision of the world was to be reinforced by still another war, this one called "Cold." It produced HUAC, blacklists, the Rosenberg trial, an air of fear made almost palpable. The message was patent: you may have emerged from nothing, but that gives you no leave to proclaim your difference, your individuality. Nor was the message lost on us. Stay vanished, place no trust in your fellow men. Only Joe McCarthy and God knew which of them were planning to destroy the system that had pulled us up from poverty and away from the brink of revolution. Your fellow men could be fellow travelers, pinkos, seeking to take away what had been regained after years of suffering and deprivation. They gave Russia the Bomb and they had hot lines to Moscow—and like as not they lived just down the hall. Why did that "nice" quiet man in apartment 6-G wear a moustache? Moustaches were not in style. A moustache . . .

If we had not already accepted a vison of the world as hostile and malignant, none of it might have happened.

Confirmed, then, was the imperative to exercise our power covertly, to surround ourselves with similar people, as near to mirror images as possible, people who would talk of anything but matters of emotional importance. In our own quiet ways we were creeping toward the aura of the power structure. We made compacts to reveal nothing, to hide feeling: we learned to talk earnestly of trivia, and what we could fully share with passion was the recipe for a dry martini.

For what our parents bequeathed us, very likely in the context of their definition of love, was a fearful self incessantly in need of support and approval in order to verify and validate its existence, its *rightness*. Afraid of open individuality, we became afraid of new ideas, of change—utterly self-centered and comfortable only with people who shared our common facade. All must remain the same, unaltered and unalterable, exactly as our parents would have it. To be special to them, to insure an approval the world denied us, we must be the constant faithful object. As the mother of a patient said to her son, "You don't need therapy. You were perfect when I had you and you're perfect now." And she meant it. He was becoming different to her.

My generation became the generation of the great narcissists, accumulating and cataloguing possessions (toys, really, since we have remained children), and we came gradually to experience the pervasive phenomenon of our middle age: the realization that when we finally have all that we are supposed to have—and my generation lives fully in the ethic of dubious imperatives— we have nothing much at all. This despite the fact that we have possessed our children as we were possessed, and it is here that the enormity of it all becomes brutally evident. Ownership has precluded understanding and sensitivity. We cannot talk with these children because we do not know them except as objects. Allegedly they are people, and so are we, yet even common language fails like the biblical babbling of tongues.

Reflection: In a music store, standing in line before the cash register, a man in his mid-forties. With him a young teen-age girl looking enough like him to be his daughter. It seemed a special day for them: they were dressed impressively, and she stared, almost trembling, as he wrote out a check for the complete hardbound edition of *Grove's Dictionary*. My fantasy was divorce, a father spending a Saturday with his daughter, a lavish, important, even spectacular birthday present. And then it happened. He asked for two receipts: the clerk wondered why. One receipt for the girl should anything be wrong with the books, the other for his accountant so he could deduct the gift as a business expense. Now what he did not see was the girl's eyes suddenly rim with tears and the delicate collapse of her features. She looked directly at him, and he at her, but apparently he saw none of the hurt, the disappointment, in the face of his tax deduction.

No, we do not know how to talk with these children. *About* them, *at* them, *to* them, but not *with* them. Because through the indifference of our self-involvement, many have slipped out of our system and are now Out There where we have never dared go. We can no longer even *see* them. The terms of ownership seem to have undergone a contractual change. At least that is how it looks—how we perceive it.

Have we learned anything from these changes? Perhaps for the most flickering of moments some of us realize that our parents failed to perform the essential function that even the lowest animal carries out with complete ease: they did not initiate us into intercourse with our larger world. They did not teach us or allow us to live with others, to touch or talk with others. They taught us to *behave*. And behavior without the inner richness of choice and feeling is the most superficial aspect of human life.

What we cannot do now is make *our* children behave, and we are floundering in the confusion of their differences from us. They have changed because of a major variation we have performed upon the theme of our parents. Whereas our parents considered us their most crucial, often only, possession, our children have come to feel that we have catalogued them as merely *another* possession, sharing parity with the color television, the automobile, the swimming pool. As we must own two televisions, two cars, so too must we own 2.2 or 2.3 children. These imperatives are taken with a seriousness that approaches morbidity. They are facts, goals, fuel, the blood of our lives.

And since these possessions are vital to us, we of course treat them well and fondle them and display them, and so many of our children are sharply aware that they are quite special—but no more special than whatever else we collect and polish in order to preserve our self-esteem via the admiration and envy of others. In short, they are despairingly aware of their price tags. They have cost us something, we have invested in them, and we want the gleam from their facets to provide a spotlight for our lives. We have tried desperately to create them in the image and likeness of ourselves. Sometimes we have succeeded, but even when we have mercifully failed, we have left them all—from the most anarchical, to the most positive, to our mirror images— with the scars of our self-involvement.

Our children of the middle class, in their late teens and early twenties, have taken several directions from remarkably similar beginnings. For a time they share our obsessions with clothing, cars, and schools that are "right" (no one really knows what goes on inside them, and sometimes a mystique is built when the admission requirement is an IQ that some administrator deems the cutoff point for a category called "gifted"). And then comes the time when lines of identity must be established. They may cast their lot with parental systems and, accompanied by adult sighs of relief and usually monetary applause, vanish in their travels along known roads. Or they stop—and here, though I simplify, two other directions are possible. One is open rebellion, the verbal condemnation of all the sacred cows of the society we have espoused, the wish to raze the entire system. They may join the tattered remnants of what has loosely been called the New Left—or the New Right or New Center or whatever else helps propel them from the parental orbit. (In my adolescence, going steady with a girl or boy of another religion—not even race—would turn the trick.) And of course the parents of my generation respond in truly predictable form: completely denying the attempt at autonomy beneath the bluster of the young rebel, and with it, denying the anger of children aimed really at parents, they fall back upon familiar ground. They blame Out There. The child has been influenced by another—by a hippie, a Jew, pornographic films, bad companions—some form of the devil, but never by parents themselves. What we do not understand is that we are quick to blame external forces only because somewhere within we are aware of how profoundly and easily *we* have been influenced.

The narcissistic wounds cut into these young people are very apparent, and, I think, less healed over than in other generations. The wounds stay raw, not fully scarred. On one hand our children are the new breed who are supposed to save society. Perhaps they may; hopefully they may. But there is a rage in them that needs to be tempered—a rage that wants to destroy anything associated with the symbols of domination and ownership, from the smashing of inanimate and quite harmless windows of city hall to the burning of a university professor's ten-year accumulation of precious research notes. These symbols seem to be substitutes for both parents and siblings. On a less dramatic activist level, the variety of our children's putdowns appears infinite; aside from themselves, no one knows anything. They quickly "invent" new modes of dress, new vocabularies, new demands; or startlingly revert to conservatism. The trappings change like sudden shifts in the wind. So they will grow, retreat, or keep on with it—and while I am no worshipper of this generation, I am aware that its members may hold the key to the future of being human. They are the living representatives of our own wishes to rebel. We have unconsciously provided a soil guaranteed to fertilize their need to find human values. Their reaction to us is the very revolt we dared not wage against those who controlled us—we, who still become eaten by guilt if we "forget" to make our weekly duty call to our parents.

But we, so vastly ignorant of what we have accomplished with our hidden wishes, suffer dreadfully in the meantime. We have created our caricature of button-down collars and noses webbed red from drinking far too many lunches, and our children are attempting to erase not just this caricature but the way of life it symbolizes. We *want* them to destroy it, and they are obeying

—at times in horribly self-destructive repudiation: the plunge into nirvana, suicide, psychosis, any sort of passive self-destruction that has near its core the paralytic inability to express anger. And even here there is going to be that kernel of grandiosity that desperately attempts to save the self from an awareness of its terrible emptiness and vulnerability. Drugs, communes in which there are enough people to prevent a focused commitment, sex without intimacy, venereal diseases—an inexorable march toward self-debasement. Often it is too late: the midnight phone call to identify a teenager dead from an overdose of ups, downs; God knows what he wanted to be, high or low, because he did not know where he was but wanted only to be somewhere else. Or the emergency room interview with a psychiatric resident trying to penetrate the phantasmagoria of a bad LSD trip.

And if the story of the girl in the music store has a poignant edge, other stories belong in a chamber of horrors, illuminating an insensitivity to our children's individual needs that crosses the threshold of madness. The man whose daughter announces her intention to become a hippie in New York's East Village —and ostensibly he calls her bluff and drives her to the train where she waves a farewell and promptly vanishes. Running away *for* him. And the parents who decided to terminate their daughter's love for her dog (apparently the only living thing that reciprocated her affection) by driving her into the desert, handing her a gun, and ordering her to shoot her animal. Whereupon she shot herself. Envious of a dog because its wagging tail undercut their ownership: and yet perhaps they really knew what the girl would do with that gun.

Ronald Laing once wrote that many of these parental atrocities are far more conscious, deliberate, than one would wish to believe,[1] and I have seen at least one instance that bears him out, though on a less spectacular level. The same male patient whose mother pronounced him perfect had as another problem an almost complete inability to achieve closeness with a woman on any level of contact. In our session his mother stated directly, and with a classical smile of smugness, that she had urged him openly and often to "stay away from girls."

An instructive example of a direct command directly obeyed, but I am after something far more subtle, which has implications for a phenomenon broader than what we might call *individual* "psychopathology." Because if that was all there was to it, simplicity would triumph; we could look for easy cause-and-effect equations, and no social problem would perplex us. What we need to examine is the fact that we shape our children largely by way of *unconscious* communications: it is their obedience to *these* that makes them so overtly different from us. How they may most *deeply* resemble us lies not in overt imitation but beneath the surface of manners, mores, values, systems. They are the handmaidens, the servants, of our unconscious desires—the desires that we fearfully keep from our awareness because they threaten us. That is why we can openly grieve and beat our breasts in public: we simply do not know that our children are carrying the banners of our own repressed rebellions. Their *behavior* is not like ours, and that is all that we are consciously aware of.

Reflection: Marcia has done everything that her parents do not approve of and no one can understand why. She is attractive, educated, and she behaves as if she wishes to drive her parents to an early grave. She openly professes bisexuality, in a current turn of the cycle has taken up with a semiliterate black man who is fond of punching her. She marches in gay lib demonstrations. Her parents are very lower middle class, have always been superior and haughty toward their contemporaries, always shooting for more status. They have disengaged themselves from their social and ethnic roots; they have legally changed their name, retaining not one trace of ethnic identification—which has caused them to invent a myth in order to explain why they know nothing of the customs of their "new" nationality.

It follows that they have always urged Marcia to be *different;*

they *lived out an example for her.* But they had no conscious idea how different Marcia would become: she rebelled, defied them, but she continues to obey them. Marcia is also different in another sense: she has come to realize that she has no conviction about what she is doing. She is not sure that she is bisexual, does not like getting beaten by her lover. Her obedience has eroded her life. Yet looking at her *behavior* we would say that her *disobedience* of solid middle-class parental values has been self-destructive. And we would be dead wrong. Except that societal norms would validate our myopia as truth.

Even this example is a rather obvious one, primarily because the life-style of Marcia's parents is so obvious. But it points to the proper direction. Children will rebel for you, destroy for you, love for you, succeed and fail for you, engage in sexual activity that you are afraid of, even kill themselves for you. It is sad that we do this, but it is sometimes the only way we can take the parental yoke off our own necks. We free our own "demons" by encouraging their release in our children; yet we are, of course, appalled when it happens. We play both sides from the middle and no one, including ourselves, knows that we are doing it. We obey and disobey our parents simultaneously; and the resultant conflict is at times shattering.

To broaden this point from the family itself, examine for a moment just one aspect of the "sexual revolution"—that is, who gives the permission for permissiveness? Who makes most pornographic films, markets them, exhibits them? Who controls the "sexual media," the magazines with their gatefolds of nudity, the sexual trade papers like *Screw* and *The San Francisco Ball?* We do: my generation. We are the ones who have inundated society with our fantasies of sexual liberation. We have put the stamp of approval on the whole business, shaking off our sexual cobwebs, our parental inhibitions—while also we make a little money out of it. We have raised voyeurism into what can only be called respectability; we want all of society to act out our trapped, damaged sexuality.

That is only a single, wider use of only one of the hidden forces within us, forces we bring to bear on our children.

I have said that all these children of the middle class have sprung from similar beginnings, and no matter what the differences in behavior seem to be, the underlying problems are going to be similar. Their narcissism prevails because there is still that inner void that we are filling with our own secret wishes. This is obvious in another preoccupation of this generation, the search for meaning in Oriental philosophies, the search for The Way. There is yoga and Transcendental Meditation, and what is similar in these mystiques is that de-emphasis of contact with others which this generation uses as a means of avoiding the experience of interpersonal anxiety. Yet despite the surface appearance of eschewing parental values, these values are acted out obliquely; crawling into oneself is also an avoidance of Out There. *Wronge*

Yet we see it all consciously, as a jarring, sometimes violent departure from our way of life, a gauntlet hurled in the teeth of our goals, imperatives, and rightness. Our children often dress like the lower classes, representative of the oppression and poverty we have clawed our way out of. They once fled to Canada to avoid the draft—scared, but not so scared that they would unquestioningly die because they were told to. They treasure music we still largely consider noise hammered out by unwashed freaks. And some even go on welfare—a beautiful irony. In short, they continue to resist some of the entrenched economic and competitive values of our culture, the very values we cling to because they define our class, our status. What they seem to have done is to have stated that they can easily render themselves valueless as possessions, and therefore socially valueless—and this demolishes our claims to ownership. They are fulfilling the deepest yearnings of our hearts, and yet we must make war on them, and they on us, as if we are two different species fighting desperately for survival. For as long as we openly oppose them, no one—not they, ourselves, nor our parents—will ever guess at the intense unspoken collusion between our generations.

And that is the true generation gap—not the stark differences between us, but the profound ignorance of our collusion. After all, if I am getting my child to live out my unseen inner life, the revelation may be terrifying for both of us—until one day when we can accept revelation for what it is: a teacher, not an adversary.

3

"Such, Such Were the Joys"

To crystallize much of what I have written about so far, I offer a long reflection that telescopes, compresses, my experiences in Catholic parochial schools. So much of my particular vision as human being, novelist, and therapist gained a rudimentary focus during those years—but, of course, at the time I was in no way aware that I was anything other than an imprisoned child. Or perhaps even that is a statement tilted awry by restrospect: I think that I was simply afraid.

Possibly I did not have to be afraid; but I was, because I had no preparation for what I would find. None of us had. Remember that we were brought up as fragile possessions, solidly paranoid about Out There. There is a faint paradox about this since at first glance a *parochial* school would seem to be tightly insulated against the great Out There. Yet the first school I attended was a perfect synonym for the kind of world our parents ostensibly wanted to shelter us from. Except that they could not see this, or did not want to. I am sure that they clung to the Church as protection against the evils and despair of everyday life.

Let me begin with a few lines from Rousseau's *Émile* as quoted (and admired) by B. F. Skinner in his *Beyond Freedom and Dignity*.[1] Rousseau maintained that a child must

> . . . believe that he is always in control, though it is always you [the teacher] who really controls. There is no subjugation so perfect as that which keeps the appearance of freedom, for in that way one captures volition itself. . . . Doubtless he ought to do only what he wants; but he ought to want to do only what you want him to do; he ought not to take a step which you have not foreseen; he ought not to open his mouth without your knowing what he will say.

If you reread this on a less obvious level, especially from half-way down, you will get the gist of my contention that parents and parental extensions often unconsciously direct their children to act out for them. And I will show how unerringly the nuns turned this trick.

But first you must know that in Rousseau's time the concept of unconscious forces was played with only by the ill-reputed darker philosophers and by churchmen sifting through problems of Satanism and exorcism. Whatever *was* acknowledged as unconscious was loosely lumped with possession; whatever it was, it was "bad." So Rousseau meant his comments in a purely conscious light (although one can sniff an unconscious working through the lines), and that is why Skinner the behaviorist can freely adopt them. To both of them, the proposition is a benign one for, as Skinner remarks, "Rousseau could take this line because he had unlimited faith in the benevolence of teachers. . . ." [2]

I was not exposed to much benevolence during my years in parochial schools, yet time has tempered the experience. Nor did those years leave me with debilitating pangs of religious guilt, a consuming dread of sin and hell, nor with a perpetual search for *spiritual* meaning, for faith. I left that world with a startling ease, almost automatically, never to return to it, never to miss it. Which raises the question, How could that be so?

The answer is simple: *I was commanded to go by my teachers.* ("He ought to want to do only what you want him to do . . .")

The overt sense of that school was something like this: My life and the lives of my peers were pillaged; we lived in constant dread of being alive. Pleasure was tension-reduction; the absence of emotional and physical pain was our pleasure. Numbness was our panacea. I personally never looked forward to the next day. Sundays were particular horrors because you were faced with five more days of school. Until I came to like what I did in life, I always had trouble with Sundays; many people have Sunday depressions. Even during the school week I stayed up late in order to drag out each tension-free moment between three o'clock and sleep.

A child should live now, look forward to tomorrow as a fresh day never before used, all days filled with discovery and adventure as well as with the pains of growing up. But we lived in despair —not something clinical like a childhood neurosis or a depression, but a dread, a despair that would lead a few of us to consider suicide as a way of shedding pain. What probably checked most of us was that suicide got you to hell; you wanted to avoid hell, get out of it, not end up there. A terrible paradox.

Suicidal? Billy, who would lie on the Long Island Rail Road tracks until he could see the face of the oncoming motorman; Andrew, pedaling his bike along Baisley Boulevard with his eyes closed; Jimmy, tattooing concentric circles on his thighs with a penknife; Edward, soaking his hand in his father's lighter fluid, firing it, then stifling it between his knees; Albert, a brilliant one, a bit put out because he didn't die from his measles in a perfect state of grace. Just kids; boys will be boys. Tom Sawyers every one.

There was nothing to do about it then but to suffer it—and perhaps with just a degree more insight into our powerlessness we might all have killed ourselves. Or others. Children must be caught young, as they invariably are.

At the age of seven I began grade 2-B at Saint Catherine of Sienna in Saint Albans, Queens, New York. The name of the school is accurate and, according to the phone book, it is still there. In fact, all the names are accurate as far as I can remember them—although there are probably thousands of Sister Mary Josephs and Sister Peters living in their anonymity.

Before Saint Catherine's I'd gone to a public school in Brooklyn, and I have little memory of that except for one whiz whose name I think was Miss Mulford. She was around sixty, and her forte was watching boys menacing other boys with their fists. And she claimed to possess a liquid which, if poured on your arm, would freeze it forever in its threatening position—a kind of perpetual impotent aggressive erection. Of course, we believed her (probably so did our parents); yet if you stopped menacing others she stopped menacing *you*—a power play with elements of fairness common to drill sergeants and other parental types who have physical streaks in their natures.

My family moved into a higher social status, from an apartment in Greenpoint, Brooklyn, to a rented house in Queens fronted and backed by small woods and flanked by two clean German-American neighbors. I bused to school; then, with the wartime fuel shortages, walked some two or three miles.

First day at Saint Catherine's: I was introduced to the class and it was pointed out (in simpler terms) that I had to be decontaminated, having spent so much time in a public school. My parents were praised because not only didn't they let me continue on in public school, but they had moved to the neighborhood because they knew how great Saint Catherine's was. (Finally I understood why we had moved. They hadn't told *me*; I guess they told the nuns.) My decontamination began with a simple question: *Who is God?* I think I said he was in the sky. And then I was slapped, a strong right-cross that drove me back against the blackboard. Like a good fighter who never wastes an opportunity, she grabbed my hair and smacked my head into the

board. Then she laughed at me and got the class to laugh with
her. Lots of overkill at Saint Catherine's.

Obviously my answer was wrong. She shoved a dog-eared
catechism in my hand: the answer was in there. Actually there
was a definite answer about who God was. I mean *definite*.
You could not, reciting back, omit a conjunction or a preposi-
tion without some implication of heresy and a suitable inqui-
sitional retribution.

Irony was, difficulty was, there *was* no God in that school; he
probably fled in a moment of panic. He was what they said he
was, and he came out mean, nasty, punitive, obsessed with
hell—totally unchristian. (Jesus had never looked mean in my
picture books: usually he was young, a halo aglow on his head;
or sitting beatifically at the Last Supper; or kneeling at some
rock.) Not once did I ever hear a word about God or Jesus that
wasn't used in the service of humiliating and beating children.
Otherwise I learned who he was through the catechism—a kind
of chairman of the board in the Andrew Carnegie mold, whom
you avoided, never opposed, and feared.

There was something else crucial about my first day: I said
nothing to my parents about it—even before I learned that a
code prevailed, a code as rigid as any code Hemingway could
construct. Boys did not tell—and the code was strictly enforced.
The nuns were glad of the code. They should have been. They
invented it.

After that first day, things fog, continuity gets lost—mainly
because, as I've said, you tried to avoid each day—and it all
boils down to a series of tormented events. And this is not all
retrospect: I can still feel the envy I felt watching the public
school kids sort of slop into school in groups, talking. At least
they *looked* free. We marched in silent lines, the punishment
for talking a slap for every word. You defended against this
angry envy with a false superiority: what price the spurious
freedom of heretics if Catholics were the only inheritors of

heaven? (As a matter of fact, there was a Protestant girl in my class, God only knew what parental aberration sent her there. She was a model child. The nuns never touched her, never even scolded her. When I first grew up I thought that the nuns were probably afraid of repercussions from the real world beyond their particular pale; but now I have a different idea.) Superiority was not only being Catholic, it was also being Irish, and not being from the Ould Sod, I was always a bit peripheral.

While the Irish never had a direct bearing on the Church except for Saint Patrick, whose day seemed more important than Christmas, the Jews certainly had. They killed Christ and enough said. I had never consorted with a Jew, but was prepared for what I *might* meet by stories told in my family of Jews stealing Catholic kids, rolling them down hills in nail-filled barrels, then using their blood in matzohs. (Obviously I extrapolated that matzohs were red.) Actually, the nuns did not much dwell upon Jews, mainly because there were no Jews around. Without the bodies you can't *really* warm to the subject. Suffice it that they, not Romans, killed Christ—although Pilate was a bastard.

No, I am wrong on one point. I had had an experience with a Jew before Saint Catherine's—a dentist who I think worked near Havemeyer Street in Brooklyn. My parents took me to him one Sunday morning. Maybe the years have resulted in a tremendous distortion, maybe the whole recollection is what the psychoanalysts call a screen memory, a "false" memory symbolic of a real, repressed event. Anyway, the way I remember it, his tools had been burglarized the night before and he had to extract my tooth with mechanic's pliers, using anesthesia that didn't seem to work. I had no feeling about the dentist, only a terror that my parents could let him do this to me. In retrospect, if you were hovering around the lower middle class in the Depression, you usually did what authority demanded: that is the context in which I perceive my parents trying to do their best. The Depression caused a lot of negative feelings toward Jews; poor gentiles bought cheap from the Jewish pushcarts on Havemeyer Street, bargaining, haggling, feeling cheated—but apparently it was the only game in town. How could they know that the peddlers were not usurers but actually barely subsisted themselves? They *owned* pushcarts. It was a logic you had to be poor to understand. But that Jewish dentist—the mind-splitting agony of that extraction, my parents' compliance—perhaps the experience was the prototype of my saying nothing about being smacked around at Saint Catherine's. My parents were accomplices. What more to say?

At Saint Catherine's you learned rules fast. Short hair was tolerated because it was clean, but they didn't really like it. It was an obstacle to grabbing hair at the temples to tug, yank, and twist. And short hair made it especially difficult for them to do something that for years made me want to hit somebody (violence breeding violence) and to this day blinds me with rage when I read of or see a battered child. The first time I saw it, it went like this:

Lined up in the hall, my class saw a boy being dangled by his hair at least a foot off the ground, a nun working over his ribs and the small of his back with her free fist, working like a piston in short forearm jabs, hammering him hard, but without a follow-through. Dangling there like a bouncing rubber doll, screaming. She pounds him and he screams, a weird muffled scream as if something soft and cloggy sticks in his throat. Some liquid, not vomit, comes through his lips. What I feel is—I wish to be not there. Not me. A crack in the floor. The filament hiding in a burned-out light bulb. It is actually the first time I pray to God to protect me; absolutely no recognition of the irony in asking him to protect me from his servants.

Dangling, he gets the fist in his stomach and falls because she lets him fall. But carefully so that his head does not strike the floor. She drags him off then, somewhere into one of those offices that always smelled like lemon oil, wax, Campbell's mushroom soup, asexuality—a place we always thought holy, a

place not to be. We always feared those offices. She drags him off.
I never see him again. He isn't one of my classmates. Later
it scares me that I never see him again. Do I think they killed
him? Soon, with the Second World War in full swing, there
would be Nazi movies; when the Gestapo took someone away
and he never came back, I would think of that scene in the hall.

Predatory birds, male birds, the nuns seemed like: black-and-
white penguins gone mad. They were time bombs. A myriad of
rules to break, to set them off.

You sat silently at a desk riveted to the floor. Sat with your
hands behind you or under your bottom or folded before you.
There was something about hands that was inherently evil, and
they were rapped almost daily with a ruler. *Your* ruler, so that
whenever you used it for its manufactured purpose—to draw a
straight line—you had a memory of being hit. A kind of primitive
feedback system. For minor infractions you got the flat of the
ruler on your knuckles; for major ones, the metal edge.

Boys were often punished by being made to sit among the girls
(segregation was rigid)—a deeply humiliating experience. Even
more humiliating for the girls when they were sent to the boys'
rows. In this little piece of sexual acting-out, the majority of
the class was permitted to titter at the outcast; thus the only
permitted mingling with the opposite sex was not born of
affection but of punishment and shame. The schoolyard was
segregated, too—an apartheid sunk deep in covert sexual fantasies.
Once a nun clamped a bow in the hair of a boy sitting in a girls'
row, and he broke down as if he had been flogged. Did the girls
feel sacrificed to a gang of juvenile rapists? Hard to know. In
grossest terms, boys were genetically bad, girls genetically harmless
if not exactly good—a motif struck in reverse by my friend Ed
Wallant, who died some years ago: in one of his novels a nun
passionately snaps that the last good man was Christ.

The nuns seemed also to realize that they could scare the hell
out of the boys by slapping one of the girls. Girls had to go very

far to be slapped, but when it happened the boys panicked. If one of the little virgins actually got clouted, what greater atrocity could *we* expect? Example-setting. Mass punishments. Often if one child was "bad" the entire class was punished—and this especially if we were due for a Christmas or Halloween party. Literally dozens of times we entered a room decorated with streamers and little baskets of goodies on each desk, only to have the party stop before it started, then sit on our hands amid the decorations, watching the little baskets collected. Maybe someone had yelped with delight before the party was officially proclaimed. Naturally we turned on the offender; sometimes one of us would beat him up after class. The art was at its greatest flower, though, when one of the girls sabotaged a party; we couldn't beat her up, only threaten. A signal lesson in impotence.

There was usually something weirdly sexual in all these goings-on, but we didn't realize it at all. When I got mine, and got it good, my sense of order and reality turned upside down. I don't quite remember what led up to it, but I think it had something to do with being accused of stealing a dime or a lollipop, or the dime to buy the lollipop. Maybe I stole it, I don't know. But Sister Mary Joseph—she had a very beautiful face—said I had and began to work me over in the hall, a flurry of open-handed lefts and rights, and suddenly I bolted and ran down the hall. She chased me; I could hear the starchy rasp of her habit, the rattling of the huge rosary beads that hung from her belt. Brilliant idea: run into the boys' toilet; she wouldn't follow me there. (I forgot who made the rules.) Inside I hardly had a moment to pant when this apparition appeared in the doorway, that absolutely beautiful face engorged. I bellowed. She worked me over some more, then slapped me into a urinal. I sat in the wet, crying I guess. Stunned. Nowhere to go, ever again. No place to run.

Of course you couldn't fight back, but you could fight each other after school. Over nothing, really; just to get it out, to unch, draw a little blood. A shot in the mouth or nose, a trickle of red, and it was all over. But it was almost every afternoon, and you got to dread the end of the day after having dreaded the day itself, especially if you were scheduled for a few rounds with someone you knew you couldn't beat. Personally, I was never really good at it anyway. The fight I won big was against a kid whose name I think was Conroy, a new kid I sort of liked. The thing got a little out of hand. We broke out of the circle surrounding us, bleeding like hell, rolling around, and at the end I gave him a real movie-type roundhouse right, but he lowered his head and my fist rammed into his skull. His head sprained my wrist and broke a small bone in my pinkie; but he cried and gave up.

Clearly we were belting the wrong people. Trouble was, we didn't know it. Hitting a nun was tantamount at least to murder, and I never saw it done. Someone could have *talked* back—a real hero, a Spartacus, a Nat Turner—but I never saw that done either.

But the organism is amazingly built to survive—partially if not completely. What many of us did was to develop a kind of negative identity, by accepting that we were as bad as they said we were. Here you could win just a little. You got, worked for, a D in conduct (red-inked on your report card), and we made it a status symbol. If you consigned yourself to the D, the junk heap of humanity, they took the pressure off. Maybe you weren't a challenge any more. A good way to insure a D, if you could take the slapping and the ruler-thumping, was by being utterly honest. Like so: you talked on line; the nun demanded to know who talked; "I did, Sister." Bang. Over a few months you could build up a solid red-soaked D, and a real high from peer acceptance. (Ds never really gave the folks at home a clue that something could be haywire; they simply assumed you deserved it.) While all this *looked* like rebellion, you were really performing an act of total obedience. They said you were bad; not only did you accept the judgment, but you illustrated, embellished, and proved it. Maybe on some level they grasped this; maybe they relaxed the pressure on the hard-core Ds out of bewilderment.

Another way of keeping them off you was to play stupid. You just didn't know. Anything. But it had to be across the board. They used to drill us in arithmetic by holding up a large metal plate with little windows in it. A five, say, would pop up in one window, a times sign in the next, and another number in the last. You gave the answer. The crucial thing was to be globally dumb at arithmetic. You had to miss every problem before they would leave you alone. Erratic performance was laziness. If you dumped every question, you were irremediably stupid at numbers and there was nothing anyone could do. That faith in genetics again.

Of course, there were kids who got everything right—usually the girls—but none of it was intelligence developed from curiosity. It was developed in the service of survival and immunity. Like the stark black and white of their habits, these nuns knew nothing of shadings, subtleties, gray areas. All was polar: good-evil, grace-sin, right-wrong. A devastating, destructive, malignant ignorance and denial of what a child is all about. And in those days nuns had had only the sketchiest of educations. They could teach only by rote. You learned it or you didn't. If you didn't, you challenged their shaky competence to the point where they had to call you hopefully dumb in order to save face.

Probably, too, they didn't want to be among children, impressed into teaching without choice, enraged at the kids because they could not admit their anger at some bishop, some superior. And destroying the impulsive spirits of children as they needed to continue destroying their own human wishes and feelings. They were, many of them, dehumanized emotional cripples.

There was Sister Gonzales—an odd name for an odd nun—who was rumored to have "nerves." She got up a project once—a monument to her eccentricity if not her "nerves." The schoolyard was ringed on three sides by wooden bleachers under which lay a decade's accumulation of dirt, leaves, and paper. She decided to clean it up. Some of us volunteered since we could get out of class. We worked under those bleachers with brooms and brushes and dustpans, and it seemed to go on forever. As rewards, she would give us some kind of Cracker-Jack candy compressed into round sticks and always stale, and she often ate it with us. When the job was done, she suddenly turned on us, took back whatever we had left of the candy, and exiled us from humanity. I don't know what we did. We saw her cry once.

One day she vanished. We turned up for school and she was gone. Tears of happiness: she was a puncher, a screamer, terrible to behold in a rage; you shook when she looked at you. Yet of all of them, she is the one I can remember with most sympathy. There was something helpless about her rages, and her sisters largely shunned her and made fun of her. She was, if not mad, somehow one of us, and I think we knew it—a madness from being trapped, a rage so great that her guilt made her want to clean up exactly that at which she was so angry.

That weird project of hers made us feel special, and it was far better under those grimy bleachers than sitting in the classroom. And her eyes were soft, without that deep glare you saw in the others'. She could never do this: send Louis, who had just shit his white knickers, to the blackboard where he had to write something while everybody watched and tittered. No, Gonzales would have screamed at him and sent him home to change. She, unlike some of the others, would not have had him dissolve in tears writing "I smell" one hundred times on the blackboard.

Nor would she have created a situation that helped George become a thief. I think it was Sister Mary Joseph who was fond of running competitions based on sales of raffle books. We were always loaded with raffle books to keep the parish solvent, and we spent a lot of our free time hounding our neighbors to buy chances. Sister Mary Joseph kept a tab on the blackboard—who was first, second, and so on. (She would also do this with straight penny-and-dime contributions.) While many of us gave our lunch money to stay in the heat of the race, George, always a loser, suddenly shot ahead with a two-dollar donation. A lot of money in those days for an eleven-year-old kid, yet no one questioned it. But I knew because George had told me: first he had been lifting change from his mother's purse, then the two dollars from his father's wallet. (Actually he had zipped ahead of *me*—I couldn't bring myself to swipe more than a dollar.) George was petrified because he had stolen the money on a Saturday night and had taken Sunday communion with the class. He was a mortal sinner, sort of waiting around to get struck dead or turn black. (We had heard the story of a girl turning black and dying the moment the host touched her sacrilegious tongue.) Of course, we were both too young to catch the irony in it all—breaking the seventh commandment to keep Saint Catherine's solvent. Maybe George had heard of Robin Hood. . . .

Finally it ended for me in the winter of 1944 when we moved to Ridgewood, Queens, a neighborhood of two- and three-floor brick houses. This time school, Our Lady of the Miraculous Medal, was literally just around the corner. I was very scared; maybe I expected something worse—but it was far better. The nuns were Sisters of Notre Dame and they rarely hit anyone; although I provoked one past endurance and she slapped me—not hard, but enough to tone down my anxiety. A smack in the head made me feel more comfortable; I knew where I stood, who I was.

By and large the nuns there were all right. Some taught by rote, others stressed music (like Sister Julia, who handed out real scores), writing themes and stories, and painting. It wasn't a bad experience, but school had already been spoiled for me. Finally I flunked out of a parochial high school and it was all over. After it all, I was traditionally fit to be several things:

...tly religious or a rebel, maybe a criminal, certainly a
and probably an eventual combination of writer and
who needed to wonder about why he turned out the

my main point: I did what the nuns at Saint
nted me to do because they could not do it
t the Church in total obedience.

us to understand that the barbarity of the good
siste   ideal ground to spawn rebellion, but such
barbar.   blamed on ignorance, frustration, whatever,
and I h   e factors their due. But the more subtle
underpinn   e that counts: so desperate was their
unconscious   Church, so desperate their denied need
to burst free   they wanted to drive children away from
God and the Church.

And of course they, and those like them, have done the job.
By brutality or apathy or ignorance—whatever the manifest
behavior—the majority of nuns and priests have ultimately succeeded in effecting their secret revolt. The Church is trembling,
its schools are in decay, entire systems of parochial education
are closing their doors. It was *this* Church that Pope John XXIII
tried to pluck from the ruins, but died before he could save.

Again I want to stress how easy it was for me to abandon
Catholicism; it was as natural as my pursuit of my parent's unconscious goals—the desire to be special in any context whatever.
Remember that I, and everyone else for that matter, had no
choice at all. We did what we were told, obeyed the powerful
secret messages. And *then* we had to struggle, as all people
must struggle. Because once the unconscious edict is obeyed and
you become what your parents and their substitutes want you to
be—well, then you must face their denial waged on a conscious
level. You *think* you have rebelled, *they* think you have rebelled,
and everyone wonders what went wrong.

And it is all based on a lack of self-awareness, which imprisons our capacity to choose and keeps us somewhat less than fully human. These days I doubt that you could find a school like Saint Catherine's in a middle-class neighborhood, but it really doesn't matter. Most systems of education, both parochial and secular, are still shaping children, slowly removing the *now* from their daily lives. Brutality is not the issue: remember that it is the unconscious message that finally counts.

Relatedness to children does get better, is more humane, as the decades pass, but the educative system still does violence to the child in order to fit him into the prevailing social norms. *All* educational systems, whether benign or malignant. This sort of training continues the overt process of parental possession by negating the moment, by guiding, always guiding, the child toward an end goal of mediocrity. The true end is a state where existential responsibility is parodied by a dependent clinging to rules, by a vocabulary punctuated by *shoulds*, *oughts*, and *musts*. Critics of education have used the battle cry that children are not permitted really to think. But more to the point is that they are rarely permitted to feel or experience themselves, so that what they wind up thinking about has very little relationship to being human. Their thinking is fixed to social utilitarianism which, as we practice it, is a vast sham, a complex net of maneuvers hiding what we really are deep within.

An example is a rather common perception of The Law. The law is an intricate system of conscious, open, codified ethics—and many people, particularly young dedicated students and attorneys, maintain that only the law has the power to change society. Whereas, in truth, it is only the *violation of laws* that fuels social change, and these violations are committed by individuals and not by abstractions. So, too, with social sham: it becomes exposed by people, not systems or mass movements, and especially by people who happen to be children. And we perpetuate the sham whose rules we still desperately need because our lives are so permeated and structured by it—rules we also wish to break with the same desperation, which is after all a main reason *why* the law exists. We perpetuate it by blocking our children's direct route to freedom and choice: their awareness of themselves, their innate capacity to be comfortably and consciously connected with their feelings and fantasies. A former professor of mine once put it this way: "You have to socialize the little bastards."

A great many children do not like to go to sleep at night, and while this maneuver is often used to avoid the next day, to escape nightmares and fears of death, even to enter a power struggle with parents, very often they don't want to sleep because, insofar as they are able, they enjoy experiencing their lives. Mostly their enjoyment of life does not occur to us. We see only the negative, talk about their health, and so on. We tell them when to live and where to live. In our jaded, defeated, fake ways, we cannot even conceive that a human being likes the experience of life.

Again, if a child is subjected to misery, he has no real awareness that this state of being is anything other than the way life is. It is not like the true narcissistic person's overblown parallel of his life to life in Auschwitz. In Auschwitz, before total numbness or psychosis set in, there was a keen, deadly awareness that cataclysm was occurring; the prisoner had a reference point, a comparative yardstick. The child, of course, has no internal reference point at all. A battered child, beaten from his earliest years, believes that all children are battered. This is also the principle by which we ostracize our "deviants": we *know* that others not like us are wrong, dangerous, or sick.

Thus a main conviction at this point: in the everyday "normal" process of losing our humanity *we haven't the remotest idea that we are losing it*. And that is why most of us rarely get in touch with what we *really* are; instead we are aware only of what we think we are, believe we are, or pretend to be. This is a frightening fact, but it explains almost everything about why, when the facade crumbles and the masks are ripped away, people tremble with the terrible, awesome posibility that there is nothing inside them, that they are empty, that they will go crazy. They will even kill to clutch back the mask, the role. Perhaps one day the ultimate in psychotherapy will parallel Alcoholics Anonymous, when the patient is asked to rise, face his fellows, and say, "I am a fake." And risk a tumble into the abyss.

To this, of course, is the counterargument that if you don't know you've lost your humanity or have played a lifelong role, then you aren't aware of having lost anything. But this is simply a more sophisticated way of culling up idiot clichés like ignorance is bliss, a little knowledge is a dangerous thing, lunatics are happy —all the clichés perpetuated as rationales for not examining ourselves, for keeping ourselves in ignorance of ourselves. It is precisely this unawareness that accounts for anxiety and depression that "comes upon" us without apparent reason, for despair, for murder, for sexual aberrations, for the insensitivities we heap upon our children—for everything that leads us to squander and destroy that which separates us from lesser animals: our humanness.

The counter-clichés are completely in the service of perpetuating society as we have known it, regardless of all the historical data that clearly underlines it as circular, unproductive, riddled with falsity, in love with mass death, stagnant, suicidal. Clichés, of course, are really the essential opiate of the masses—those large groups of people, the common man, the silent majority, who are always, in good American tradition, supposed to "come through." Except that they are kept in abject ignorance, not from the *news*, but from themselves—a primary way that we have brought up our children. We have raised them to be unaware of themselves, to obey any parental whim or edict simply because it emanates from the parent—and so, even in "democracies" we need a parental figure on top who metes out rewards and punishments. God is too metaphysical, too invisible: we need a President who, like our parents, can call us "fellow Americans," but who is clearly superior to us. We no longer even know that we are being patronized. Having been so thoroughly conned, so thoroughly raped, we know no other way.

It begins at home and it extends to the institutions we permit to sponge up our children. Which of course was a prime reason why I never told my parents about the beatings at Saint Catherine's. To me, a child, this is what I thought education was (I didn't grasp that *learning* was something quite different until I bumped into one teacher in my senior year in high school, a poet and great teacher, who, like a great parent, had the knack of simultaneously propelling you onward and getting out of your way). I never told them, because the school, the nuns, *became* them, *were* them. They had sent me there. In assuming their correctness, perhaps even their omnipotence, it was the logical equation to make. And of course, despite the D in conduct, I did not *really* want them to consider me a "bad" child; after all, that was why I was being smacked around. To make me "good."

And if I have not become what my parents wished me to be (though in truth I *have*), if I have slid away from the Church and cast a suspicious eye on any authority that crossed my path —well, it was because of that very logical equation. It has been difficult to sort out. But, although it has components of a psycho-analytic transference, where one person is unconsciously viewed as possessing characteristics of another, there has been enough commonality in our parents, our teachers, our bosses, our Presidents, to make this a phenomenon that transcends transference. The larger truth is that past generations have indeed been more alike than not. This is what has given our society the sameness that passes as continuity. If we react to parents and teachers and certain kinds of bosses and certainly most Presidents in somewhat the same way, then I call this reality. Only when we insist upon reacting this way to a person who is not truly in the mold is it truly transference and on some level of self-destructive; but if we do not view authority with suspicion, then we are flirting with incredible danger. We are then apt to "adjust," to say "life is like that," to lose our identity and become pawns, fools, or, with enough money, some human variety of cow searching for contentment. Searching to fill both levels of our narcissistic emptiness: others must applaud us for our social face; yet still others must satisfy our craving to be free, impulsive, wild. We will adjust on the surface and live our real lives through others.

4

Living Unconsciously
Through Others

I have used the terms *narcissism* and *narcissistic* in referring both to my generation and to our children, and what I mean by them is really little more than a shorthand to describe people whose basic makeup leads them to live through others or to get others to do something for them. Narcissistic behavior ranges from deliberate, planned manipulation to the kind of unconscious molding of our children that I have been trying to describe. In either case the narcissistic person attempts to seize, con, or wheedle something he needs from another human being—and the needs can be physical or emotional, conscious or unconscious. He may attempt to steal an identity.

Decades ago we called such a person "selfish" and let it go at that. Today narcissism is a booming business in psychiatric and psychoanalytic circles. Books and papers are being turned out, therapists and supervisors hunt meticulously for "narcissistic features" in the patients with whom they deal. Rollo May suggests that patients' problems predict future social trends,[1] but actually they mirror what is happening now, perhaps in its most acute form. We are becoming afraid of our narcissism, which is why it is being pushed into the psychotherapist's office. Once there, it gets labeled as a sickness and we can stand back from it; it becomes part of the alien Out There. But standing back from it is impossible because it is really a far broader cultural phenomenon than a mere psychiatric entity.

Like all stages in development, narcissism is an ordinary step in the process of becoming human. But in our culture—particularly in the society forged by my generation—it seems to have arrested and solidified. Instead of being the beginnings of a transition from self-preoccupation to the establishment of meaningful and open relationships with others, it becomes no such intermediary stage at all. Rather it is a fixation, which damages the capacity for human touch and undermines the sense of possessing a self, an independent self. It permeates every aspect of the character. It is not some isolated symptom; the symptom is the entire personality—and with enough of such personalities a social character is formed.

In his book, *On Adolescence*,[2] Peter Blos cites the boy who masturbates less frequently as a result of his growing involvement with a girl, as he begins to make the transition from sexual self-involvement to what psychoanalysts call a "love object" —which simply means a person with whom we fall in love or to whom we show affection. Our love is directed outward, which may lead to a bond of mutuality should the other person reciprocate. Ideally this is the heaven where good marriages are made. But the narcissistic person does not make this transition; in varying degrees of severity the capacity has been short-circuited. The other person is valued not as a lover with his own integrity, but solely as an object in the more common meaning of the word, an external object that performs the masturbation, that exists only to service. With a dazzling ease, the narcissist can move on to someone else, with no emotion or sense of loss, since all people are more or less interchangeable. A human being must be important, even in some way unique, if his loss is to be felt, and people are simply not important to the narcissist unless they exist solely to satisfy needs.

Because of the dehumanization implicit in this way of being in the world, it is difficult to penetrate the overt behavior and attempt to sympathize with the inner lives of narcissistic people. There is almost no way in which to describe them without shading into some form of character assassination. They are vain, haughty, preoccupied with at least some aspect of physical appearance—though it does not have to be the traditional image of staring lovingly into a gilt-framed mirror. There are also traditional labels other than selfishness: self-love is one, and, more recently, ego-tripping. But on the dark side of the mirror, this self-involvement is born of a terror that nothing exists within. It is a mutilated self trying desperately to establish itself as the center of a vast universe of emotional filling stations, an only child in a world of accommodating, admiring adults. It is an emptiness searching for euphoria and praise without the necessity of commitment. Commitment cannot be made on an emotional level because human relatedness has never been experienced except in some context of ownership.

In purest form, and it is rarely completely pure, narcissistic people are unlikable and so alienating that no one with whom they come in contact has the charity to take into account the depletion of their humanity. Promised everything useless or fantastical (like the paper economy of the last generation), they were given only unobtainable grandiose dreams, and so they may appear superior and superficial, chronic complainers who justify their misery by excoriating societal forces—often with accuracy. Since the good things in life are entitlements—and we shall see later why this is so—only the injustices are remembered and are woven into a tight fabric of resentment, bitterness, and deprivation. These people are corrosively envious, because by some process of vague magical thinking whatever *you* possess deprives *them*. You must satisfy them totally or they cannot be satisfied at all. They seem active but are profoundly passive, like crying thrashing infants who scream for food but who must wait until it is given. They are ethical only to reproach and accuse others. In relating to them you have no integrity or identity, you cannot feel vital, because they have psychologically murdered you. Your feelings, ideas, and plans are of no importance. If you honestly wish to help them, to give of yourself—and this has been the experience of every psychotherapist I know—you feel helpless and impotent because nothing you do is good enough. From the bedrock of their resentment emerges a need for revenge; and one of its goals is to frustrate and thwart whatever comes close.

At their most driven, they will manipulate, exploit, lie, cheat, even steal in their pursuit of what they need.

Reflection: She brings her bundle of laundry into the basement, drops it into the machine, jams her quarter into the slot. There is no one in the basement, but she notices her neighbor's laundry cart waiting by a drier. She notices it because she notices everything about her neighbor, who is young, beautiful, married, apparently a happy woman. Her lip curls slightly, something that feels a bit like an electric current tingles her hands and lower spine, and she quickly peers out into the dim corridor. Empty. And quickly, she jerks open the drier, plucks out a pair of bikini panties, and shoves them into her blouse. Excited, but with an excitement, a momentary fulfillment that will soon pass, she leaves the basement in triumph.

No one knows that this woman steals selected little objects that fill her up when she needs refueling; no one knows how resentful she is, how enraged and vindictive. She hides herself well. No one knows that her husband left her because he could not live with her jealousy and envy. Acquaintances think she has been victimized. She seems a model mother to her young daughter.

This woman's overt behavior is an example of why so many narcissistic traits are not seen by others. They are often tempered and masked by charm, ostensible honesty, pretended interest (on some level you probably think that they are doing something for *you*), and precisely when you wish to further the relationship—it ceases. Probably such people have felt that some expectation of them has been kindled; or that you have disappointed them. For them you are always either too much or not enough, idealized or devalued, but you are never yourself, never real. You have no mobility in the relationship unless it is perceived that you are supplying something needed. But they are perpetually looking for a better deal elsewhere.

Of course there is a continuum among narcissistic people as there is among paranoid people: narcissistic behavior can range from abjectly intolerable to somewhat acceptable, as a delusion can be malignant or relatively benign. And aside from the core of outright con men, most narcissists realize that in order to get something, they dare not alienate others entirely. Actually narcissists often get along exquisitely with each other if there is a lot of mutual stroking and preening free of emotional commitment and demands. They are swingers, jet-setters, fun people —the Beautiful People. And it is very like the parallel play of young children: they are not really *with* each other, they are merely in the same playpen.

The key, really, is that narcissistic people do not experience a full complement of their available human emotions, and much of what they do feel is particularly one-sided in their contact with others. If there is happiness, it is the unshared contentment of being admired, praised, and respected—respect always being a substitute for love. The negative feelings are *truly* intense: disappointment, resentment, envy, hurt, wounded pride, and a chronic anger rooted in an unending frustration. These feelings are always perceived as caused by you: your unkindness, cruelty, lack of consideration, neglect. Narcissistic people, when they feel even remotely slighted, can easily compare themselves—and quite seriously—with the Jews of Auschwitz and the dissidents of Torquemada's Inquisition.

Again, it is a pity that a narcissistic person cannot be described *behaviorally* in positive terms; for this reason the negative feedback he frequently receives confirms his view of the world as an unjust, mean place. Yet often his role is accepted. He can be a film star, a corporation president, President of the United States. He can be a musical genius like Richard Wagner, though our age is notoriously and woefully short on Wagners. These are the socially and economically successful people; and we tend to view them firmly within their roles, since their roles appear to be their identities and we all admire success. Thus we talk of the presidency or the papacy as offices that "elevate" the man—a piece of nonsense that the younger generation is undermining with explosive force.

Despite the cosmetic veneer of success, the basic person remains. You cannot sympathize with the obvious pain of his psychosis because he is not psychotic. Nor can you appreciate the strains of his debilitating compulsions or his dangerous spells of fainting—because he isn't prone to them. You usually cannot get at the deeper roots of his being—the profound deprivation of real affection, the unrealistic expectations planted within him, his need to deal with others as he has been dealt with, all autonomy stripped away by parents who possessed him in order to enhance themselves. Because all this basic dehumanization and the laming weakness it implies, is masked by a defensive self-inflation, a false aloofness and hauteur designed to protect the needy, vulnerable inner child from even more hurt, disappointment, and manipulation. He is really saying, "I need you so much that I dare not need you." Consequently, he would rather manipulate, con, steal, extract than allow you the "power" to see his real needs. In his world, the needy man, who by definition is the man down, is kicked in the face or urinated upon.

So far my descriptions imply a *you*—the observer—and a *he* or *they*—the narcissist. Such splits are obviously artificial, though generally comforting, and creep into our descriptions largely as the result of our obsession with the "scientific" method. These splits serve the cause of pseudo-objectivity and are, ultimately, probably useful only in attempts to study mankind in the most trivial of its facets—such as nail-biters versus non-nail-biters. A microscope, with man fixed to the slide, gets us off the hook of identification; we pretend that the person we observe and react to, especially if we see him in a negative light, is not at all like us (the President is, or may be, like us; the *man* who has been "elevated" *by* the office we may violently dislike). All human encounters based upon this dubious split usually remove us from an understanding of ourselves, but here I make the split deliberately, precisely in order to stimulate an identification. Not an identification with the narcissist Out There, but the identification with the narcissist within. And much of this book will stress this identification and examine it deeply. Because it is our narcissism, our inner void, that propels us to have our children act out for us, to have them do what we dare not.

Also important to my purpose in describing the narcissistic character is that, by and large, the narcissistic person is not aware of these traits as many of them have taken on a patina of social value—spurious though it may be. They are components of success in a culture gone berserk with success, gone berserk with driving faster and harder purely for the sake of the gooseflesh inherent in its own frenetic motion, where to pause and reflect courts the danger of suffering insight into the signal failure of our fantasies and dreams. A cultural agreement has been forged: we give the appearance of productivity through perpetual motion and perpetual consumption as substitutes for feeling and self-awareness, for insight and sensitivity. Our narcissism has dulled us to the needs of those closest to us; and one day the center falls apart.

Of course, I am saying that my generation is a narcissistic generation without peer in this century, unequaled in its ability to hide its inner void with the trappings of success, money, power, possessions. Unequaled, too, in its utterly fantastic ability to get its children to live for it, to fill the void—and then to be startled by the results, to attempt to seal up what we have unconsciously set loose. A teen-ager becomes a Jesus Freak out of some desperate search for meaning, whereupon we hire a bona fide freak to "debrief" him. And all the while he is simply trying to find the meaning that also eludes us but that we would never dream of pursuing outside the framework of what we were trained to believe. We send him out to discover something, then ambush his discovery as soon as it exceeds the comfort level of our fear. Again, using the broader social phenomenon of the "new" sexual permissiveness, the reaction against it will be waged by ourselves—we who created it. We let some impulse out of our hermetically sealed vaults, then get too frightened and crush it. And we may also tighten up on any inner violence that we have commercialized in the media.

This must be the crucial difference between ourselves and our parents: they have been relatively satisfied with our performance, because our freedom as individuals was successfully thwarted and we remained deeply dependent upon them. We want the permission of our parents to be free but cannot obtain it. They still literally tell us how to live, how to behave, and despite our anger and despair we obey. And so we try to set ourselves free through the "wildness," rebellion, and disobedience of our children. We give our children subliminal permission so that *we* can feel that *intense thrill* of identification with their impulsivity and disdain of authority and traditional values. That we are appalled is an unconscious con game—because whatever we have gotten them to do accrues to *us*, and therein lies the deepest stratum of my generation's narcissism. We are the great manipulators of the unconscious.

In psychotherapy the manipulations sooner or later become apparent—and so do the unconscious forces that propel them. But that is not why members of my generation come to therapy, to uncover what they are unaware of. They come often out of their passivity, an inability to act; and they come because they are not *happy*, not gratified. In short, they come to find just a little bit of magic, and the therapist is the magical parent.

Typical of my generation is that if you have a problem you lay it in the hands of a psychotherapist; you foist it on him; you bring it to him like a surly dog on a dangerously frayed leash. Despite our emphasis on motion, work, busyness, we wait for tragedy as if we own a block of tickets for the Greek theater, next performance time unspecified. We "find" ourselves in destructive marriages; our children are mysteriously "different"; things *happen* to us. In any way available we try to minimize our responsibility. This sort of passivity and helplessness is inevitable wherever links are not made with human beings but with things or people treated as things. Thus *things* go awry, do not work out, happen to us.

And the young people? The young people come because they cannot feel who they are, aware that they have been treated as possessions, frightened because they don't understand why they do what they do, genuinely frightened by a lack of will and choice. They know that something is wrong, and it has to do with an inability to feel fully and to enjoy contact with others. Indeed, many of them can crystallize exactly what I am saying when they lament that they have no idea if what they feel "belongs" to them or to their parents. This is a far cry, a light-year away, from the complaints of the past, which centered on conflicts around direct obedience or sexual problems or phobias. These young people don't know whose feelings, whose unconscious, they are expressing. When they come in contact with others, they simply don't know.

It is this group whose reactive quest for dynamic change,

whose sudden search for emotional experience, may cause us, if we are open, to reassess the idea that the absence of real relatedness, the condition we have come to label as apathy, is the natural way of contemporary man.

5

The Tyranny of the Ego
and the Subversion of Now

Now we can refocus narcissism in a particular way, not merely
as overt selfishness or a psychiatric illness or a cluster of obnoxious
character traits. We can redefine it as a need to manipulate
a person in order to gratify oneself on several levels simultaneously. Such a way of operating, usually with our children, must
produce intense inner conflict because the levels of gratification
may be diametrically opposed. I have already hinted at this in
Chapter II with Marcia, the girl who is "different," who seems
to be driving her parents to an early grave because she obeys
while overtly disobeying. Simply put, a parent's attempt to play
both ends from the middle generally fails: a parent's conscious
wish that his child reflect social glory and toe the line is in
conflict with his unconscious wish that the child act out his
rebellion for him. What results is that both parent and child
are disappointed, confused, torn apart. The unconscious message,
I repeat, is always the strongest, and it will be this message that
propels the behavior that frightens us.

Ironically, my generation's manipulation of its children's unconscious in order to free its own is a tremendous struggle to
find humanness, for the unawareness of our inner forces is
precisely the ignorance that prevents us from living fully as
human beings. If we do not know what we are, then we can
only live a life of approximation: we are something *like* human
but not completely so. This particular sort of ignorance is utterly
obvious: it expresses itself each time we "don't know" what
troubles us or why our children behave as they do. And yet it is
perfectly within our grasp to know; how can we *not* know? We
are not one species trying to solve the riddles of another, nor
are we faced with the job of analyzing the personalities of beings
flown to earth from some strange planet. But certainly we usually
act as if we can never know ourselves.

The answer, I think, lies in the fact that we have tyrannized
ourselves with false "knowledge"—shaky concepts invented to
explain and rationalize what we are. How poor these concepts
are is apparent by how they crumble over the ages: astrology has
a modern following but is hardly flourishing as it once did; traditional religion is floundering badly; accepted forms of social
order turn chaotic with mind-boggling ease. But perhaps the
most damaging idea is that life *must* involve intense suffering
and that we *must* put off experiencing the immediacy of the
process of living—that is, that life has some huge purpose instead
of being a span of time in which the only requirement is simply
to live. In essence, we have tried to stifle the present, deny *now*,
as if that were necessary to achieve a secure future. We are
obsessed with knowing the future when it is a thing we cannot
know—but it is an idea that *must* obsess us so long as we avoid
feeling life as an ongoing process. We have been taught to use
now only as a step to get somewhere else. Yet living now, fully
in the present, is the single means by which we can contact
ourselves, feel—and, ultimately, know ourselves so that vicarious
living may cease. It is really a very simple proposition: the more

fully one lives, the less need to live through others—both consciously and unconsciously.

What has happened to the concept of now? Something odd indeed. Since the advent of civilization more or less as we know it today, now has become a suspect, even a feared, moment of time. It has been seen as the province of young children and the "lower classes," whose alleged search for on-the-spot gratification is supposed to be immature and impulsive. The spectrum ranges from a child's "evil" glee as he smears his feces to a muscled dock worker's life goals of screwing, boozing, and brawling. (Middle-class people, of course, do none of these things: they make love, drink socially, and quarrel.) Children, we *think* we acknowledge, are children—though they must be whipped into line—while the "lower classes" are a mixed bag of blacks, Puerto Ricans (before them the hot-tempered vitriolic Italians now canonized by the commercialized Mafia industry), Chicanos, Sioux, whatever. These "classes" are really the products of Anglo-Saxon-Judeo-Christian alchemy, created from the deadness of emotions atrophied in the service of hard work, thrift, and the occult mysteries of the future.

Always there has been something *wrong* with people whose desires are present-oriented: the black man of mythic sexual lusts intent on conquering a white woman (*any* white woman), the rebel who seeks social reform *now*. The labor unions, once rabid exponents of now, have moved with startling ease from militancy to establishmentarianism. Once the CIO had its "left foot forward"; now union men beat up youthful demonstrators. But they are not impulsive; an ex-president and an ex-vice-president said they weren't.

Now is clearly "bad," we have defined it as such, and we will embrace any philosophy or psychology that sacrifices it, that frowns upon it. I have said that psychoanalysis grew extremely popular in this country after the great stock market crash; probably it was a kind of Westernized yoga, a way of deemphasizing the pain and frustration of everyday life. Psychoanalysis deified the concept of ego and lent us *intellectual* tools to understand the human being—highly intellectual tools. But ego is the backbone of psychoanalysis, a backbone literally lifted from centuries of entrenched social values. Actually it is absolutely medieval.

Ego is supposedly the mediator of reality, an agency of the mind that arbitrates and compromises between our usually unconscious primitive wishes and the limitations of external (social) codes or possibilities. It is not what the layman usually calls it —something that is enhanced or puffed up by praise or positive feedback. (Indeed, the narcissism that this generation subliminally recognizes in itself has led to the invention of the term *ego-trip*.) According to theory, the sounder the ego, the more a person is reality-based; hence the healthier he is, the more appropriately he behaves. One of the crucial points here—and the one I am emphasizing—is that the gratification of so-called infantile wishes and needs must be delayed. The future, though nebulous and unknown, is supposed to be all: the ego is the mental structure that permits a person to spend some twenty-five years in school in order to achieve a professional goal. It also permits him to save money so that he may retire to the graveyards of Florida at age sixty-five. In sum, when you are firmly ego-oriented you live at a certain level of what might be called deprivation, tolerating frustration in order to reach any long-range end—this end naturally being one approved of by traditional social codes. (The process must be suffered.) Yet if a man carefully plans a robbery for ten years, and then successfully brings it off, his ego is not considered healthy; he is called a psychopath. (To many of us he is a hero, judging by the smashing box-office successes of "thief" films. Con men to the last, all of us, but we would never really slide the pearls off the neck of the duchess. We just make the movies.)

Of course, there is no such thing or entity or structure as the ego. It is a rationalization aimed at explaining and justifying why we put up with so much deprivation to achieve social value. It is patently in the service of perpetuating social obsolescence: it justifies our sadism—for example, beating students as an aid to learning, which in turn is necessary if they are to succeed in "real life." (In recent years we have become corporally humane; the whips and rods are now such things as Graduate Record Examinations, Scholastic Aptitude Tests, etc.)

Simply put, you get enough people ostensibly to agree on a definition of reality or the sanctification of a goal, and you may do what you damn well please to push your children in that direction—beat them, starve them emotionally, whatever. If they object or rebel—well, they are like the patients who belligerently refuse to respond to psychoanalytic treatment. They lack ego.

While theorizing about the ego and its complexities has resulted in a school of psychoanalytic thought called Ego-Psychology, the ego simply does not exist except as an idea. Also, it has nothing at all to do with psychoanalysis. The concept of ego is fundamentally a religious abstraction. In most forms of Protestantism it justifies the Puritan ethic of hard work and thrift; in Judaism it "explains" the oppression and persecution of chosen people who must wait for redemption and reward—but who now, via the incredible skills of the Israeli army, are beginning to act as if it is better to live today, and who, by this position, are consequently annoying the world community. But Christianity, especially Catholicism, extended the concept further: the process of living is a process of suffering, or at least a process in which natural gratifications, such as sex, are deliberately drained of pleasure—and in the service of achieving the greater rewards of an afterlife, of heaven. In any case, the process of living must be sacrificed for the sublime end-goal. Aside from political implications, this is called hope. But polarities, opposites, however untenable, are vital to perpetuate the system: the joys of heaven versus the horrors of an eternal hell; social success versus skid row; a functioning ego versus some form of insanity or unacceptable impulsiveness.

With Freud, we have codified into a psychological "truth" what has always existed as a social crutch: the concept of ego is a justification for the assumed pain of living; and this is only one point at which the orthodoxy of psychoanalysis dovetails with the orthodoxy of religion.

What the present generation rebels against—and the grandiosity of narcissism aids rebellion, for you must feel *right* to revolt —is the monstrous domineering ego of its parents and of anyone else who consciously plays the old-line parental role. This generation of parents has acted out the rules of the ego to the point of caricature and self-parody—and therein lies the evidence of its basic insincerity. It stresses the achievement of some goal which is ultimately perceived as meaningless. And this is what I have called the tragedy of my generation: the recognition, usually in middle age, of a deathlike stagnation after years of frenetic motion without content, without gratification. We have lived in the past and we have lived for the future but we have excised the everyday process of our lives as if it were a cancer.

Reflection: At forty-three Bernie is high-powered, success-oriented, sharp, driving, handsome, charismatic. He has captured more accounts in six years than his public relations employers have witnessed in two decades. They make him a senior vice-president, the youngest man ever to hold the position. He is so elated he trembles; he is near the very top. Quite consciously he looks into a mirror and says what he once said at his Bar Mitzvah: "Today I am a man." This is a Friday and he celebrates with his wife at the most expensive French restaurant in New York—perhaps in the whole country, the whole world. By Monday morning Bernie can barely get out of bed; he has never been so depressed. He is immobile; his arms, legs, and head feel like stony weights; talking is an agony. For the first time in his life he has suicidal thoughts. They won't go away: a leap from a window, a razor drawn across his wrists, pills. By the end of the week he is almost mute, but he manages to tell his wife: *I can't take forty-three more years of it. I can't. Please, I can't.* Tears roll down his cheeks. Finally he says nothing.

Bernie is given a series of six shock treatments; there are a few weeks of haziness afterward; then he seems to get it together. His bosses never mention the episode. Nor does he. He continues to bring in accounts. He seems to do everything twice as fast now.

Bernie is certainly not the rule. But he is not really an exception either. Some level of himself simply realized that the entire thrust of his life was aimed at validating a stereotype, an illusion. In the process he forgot to live. *I can't take forty-three more years of it,* he says. He experiences that he has been doing what he has been doing since the day he was born. And the *Please?* From what great power is he begging release? Perhaps he would rather kill himself than go on dying. But the shock fixes everything: the electricity short-circuits his awareness and any possibility of using it to change himself. It punishes him for transgressing against "reality," for questioning his inner forces, and for his own good it brings him back to where he was. No, wait—now he does everything twice as fast.

Bernie might after all kill himself if he can get depressed enough while he is still doing everything twice as fast. He might want to fly off a bridge or swim the Atlantic.

Where are you now? What are you feeling now? Perhaps a pair of the most anxiety-provoking questions one can ask because *most of us have no now*—and this lack of in-touchness is precisely what young people cannot tolerate. Rightly so, since the elusiveness of *now* is really at the root of what is called the lack or loss of identity. An identity crisis—another term much bandied about—is merely the panicky awareness that one cannot account for one's presence in present time; hence "depersonalization," where you seem to watch yourself since you cannot or dare not feel.

To counterclaim that an emphasis on now results in hedonism or anarchy (which behind the abstract words usually means sexual play and independence) is to miss the point and is simply a reflection of the difficulty in grasping the reality of present time, a reflection of how assiduously we have avoided the present, a reflection of how frightened we are of it—because having dug it out of our lives, it is a yawning hole. What it truly means, this experience of now, is an awareness of being alive at the moment; and so difficult is this awareness, so alien to the way we have always been, that new methods of psychotherapy—actually, new methods of relating to ourselves—have evolved to facilitate it.

Yet there is another sort of now of which my generation is quite fond: consumerism, impulse buying, the Great Sale that generally offers what nobody needs. This kind of now has an almost complete social imprimatur, since a lot of people make a lot of money by manipulating impulsiveness, just as a lot of money is jangling into the tills of the porno industry. To commercialize anything is fine because one of our long-range ego goals is dazzling affluence.

But the "destruction" of the ego leaves open the possibility of immediate gratification of another kind. The quest for gratification is logical since, owned by parents and their surrogates, children were and are forced to delay the gratifications to which they have a legitimate right—that is, to be fed when *they* are hungry, to wear warm clothing when *they* are cold, to be held when *they* need holding, to express strong emotion when *they* feel it. Narcissistic people, even in adulthood, continue to search for the gratification of their needs while they are experiencing these needs. Thus their feeling that they are *entitled* to the "good things," which appars as haughtiness and ingratitude, is merely a way of stating that what they never received as children—the legitimate gratifications—they now accept as a bona fide birthright, much as a hungry infant experiences no need to offer thanks for a feeding. The satisfaction of a natural organic need is, or should be, a quite ordinary experience. Few people expect an infant to bow and scrape after a trip to the breast or bottle. It will only be the negative that the child will violently respond to: the empty breast, the unavailable breast, or—more subtly and more common—the breast that is provided in conformity with the mother's schedule and not in response to her child's needs.

Hence, people will tend to take for granted the gratification they feel legitimately entitled to, which expressed by an adult appears to be grandiose and "egotistical"—in short, narcissistic—the acceptance of birthright as if it were the expression of the divine right of royalty.

Now we can begin to understand why the narcissistic person, and the narcissist within us, looks so unpalatable: as an adult he accepts with aplomb those positive offerings, now symbolic, that had he received as a child he would have unemotionally accepted as the ordinary byplay of a sound relationship with his parents. The intense emotions, especially frustration and anger, occur when these ordinary gratifications are withheld, suddenly removed, or capriciously given—capriciously as felt by the child, even though the parents might view themselves as paragons of consistency.

So the narcissistic person, in attempts to get or to make up for what he lacks, plumbs his repertory: he demands, fawns, sponges, cons, cheats, manipulates, rips off. And he does so because he believes that his needs cannot and will not be met by honesty and legitimate requests. Since they have not been met honestly and directly in the past, why should he assume that they will be met now or in the future? But this wheedling and even dishonest attempt to get something has a positive element: the person has not given up all hope for gratification (the world may still have something to offer), thereby sinking into a chronic depression or malignant withdrawal. There is *still* a belief that others have something to give even if they will not give it freely. Faith in people still exists: thus the narcissist insists that usual ways of human interaction must change in a more positive direction (even if this strongly implies his own enhancement), and his grandiosity dictates that he can to some degree effect the change. And this is what seems to be happening today. We are historically used to the spectacular changes wrought by spectacular narcissists—Wagner in music; Napoleon in politics and warfare; Edison in technology—ad infinitum. But we are simply not used to the idea that the "ordinary" narcissist can effect anything of significance, and so we continue searching for gratification through our children.

Yet *they* are desperately, and I think often meaningfully, searching for both themselves and us, aiming at awareness and feeling. The center of their target, the emotional bull's-eye, is the present —the "Now Ethos," a term apparently coined by Erving and Miriam Polster,[1] two prominent Gestalt therapists. To my mind it is the most significant ethos adopted by young Americans in this century. It has nothing to do with impulse buying, and does not even have a root in the jazz age of the twenties, where naughtiness found the propelling media of so-called jazz music and bootleg booze, and which in any event was the province of the rich whose traditional values lurked only an inch or so beneath the facade of playboy and flapper. It is an ethos that has forged many of the current psychotherapeutic modalities, particularly Gestalt, Encounter, and to some extent Primal Therapy, and it has created its own place, its own Riviera—Esalen in California. And it raises the vital question of whether these new modalities are really psychotherapies or simply ways to bring people to higher levels of personal awareness. This is a knotty proposition: the stimulation of "awareness" can range from the pitiable and false idea that the dilemmas of women emanate exclusively from male oppression to the profound truth that a human being is his own keeper. Ultimately, the Now Ethos must be the underpinning of all life if there is going to *be* a future in which to be human.

The now phenomenon goes on, smashing through class and institutional barriers, given its thrust mainly by very middle-class young people who are clearly frightened of traditional futures and dubious delays. I am going to offer a social hypothesis here which at first glance may seem startling—but who can tell? Oppressed groups like the blacks have been denied a legitimate now just as the young middle class has been denied one—but for blacks, deprivation is double-barreled. They have been robbed simply by being children in this society; and they have been robbed once more by being black children in this society. But their blackness will be the point of sharpest focus, since blackness is the most obvious fact. That is, most blacks want the social benefits from which they have been traditionally excluded while the young middle class disavows them although for them they are definitely within reach.

White youth wants emotional freedom, something they have always romantically envied about the black world—the "soul," the apparently improvisational quality of daily life, the music. (Only from this generation could a Janis Joplin emerge, a white girl who sang like a black girl and who died the death of a whole despairing black culture.)

My hypothesis? If blacks continue to gain the traditional benefits of society while white youth continues to search for inner awareness outside societal boundaries, blacks will become the new Puritan middle class. In the process they may lose, then need to regain, their "soul." Whites, though a numerical majority, will be off somewhere, peripheral people. A staggering social reversal. We are a long way from the day when blacks are able to identify themselves as human beings pure and simple.

With whites, there is no product involved in their new ways of attaining feeling and emotional awareness, the capturing of now —and the new therapies reflect this. Conversely, in psychoanalysis, as in all our traditional institutions, a product is always implicit in its stress upon adjustment to social "realities": accept society and it accepts you with its "real" rewards.

The quest for feeling, for the experience of now, admittedly has a utopian ring. Yet the utopianism seems a bit more convincing than in times gone by since this generation has begun its drift away from dreams of communes and the hope for truth through acid. It sweeps more broadly, it becomes more personal, it begins to work from inside outward: something is being brought *to* experience, and that is the nub of social change. Much of this generation really believes that the experiencing of now is the key to curing most of the world's ills, to breaking the destructive patterns of the past. Hence their working to death of the word *relevance*. And there is a profound truth in this view despite its occasional excessiveness. Our way of life is historically, socially, politically rooted in deadly repetitions which appear to doom our world but which really consign it to a circular stagnation—in terms not of technology but *of its almost absolute unconcern with human growth and spiritual fulfillment*. There has never existed one large-scale social *institution* that has seriously held individual human worth as a prime value. The individual has never counted in the societal structure except in lip service. The only effect of Santayana's admonition about the perils of historical ignorance has been to help lengthen the pages of volumes dedicated to the collection of proverbs and pithy quotations. Society will not move; only individuals will move. Society takes comfort in repetition, since repetition absorbs the potential anxiety of change—which is why our leaders always seek to *unite* us in some common cause of this year's invention, whether it be the lowering of thermostats to conserve energy or the paranoid vision of encroaching Communism. If now our society is not united—then *bravo*. It does not mean *torn apart*. It means that individuals may be waking from the stupefaction of collective apathy.

Our Western society, as Freud clearly saw[2] but chose not to contest, is based primarily, if not exclusively, upon sublimations of what we are really all about. It stresses what we should become, not what we are. We are trapped in time because we venerate the past, thus making the past identical to the future. If the future will be the same as the past, then we can face the unknown without fear. In essence, to preach the importance of the future is to ask for a direct line to the past. A retreat into the past is generally called a regression, a remaining in the past, a fixation—and I maintain that a preoccupation with the future is no less a regression or fixation since the future is "deciphered" for us. We can pretend to know it precisely because we predicate its content upon what we have done in the past. This is our time-trap, the quintessence of the coda to a small prayer which goes "as it was in the beginning, is now, and ever shall be, world without end. Amen." Amen, indeed. If there is a death instinct, it is this: not a drive toward literal death, but a driven necessity to remain stagnant. And what remains stagnant rots, like a corpse.

Scaling this down from the mass social level to its component parts—individuals—we learn a great deal from "patients" if we let them lead us into the uncharted waters of their lives instead of forcing them to conform to our theories. And we learn a great deal from young people, patients or not. Risk of any sort—anger expressed toward a parent, changing jobs, relating or perceiving in any different way—is feared because of some fantasied future calamity. For example: "If I did that, he would. . . ." No one *truly* knows what *will* happen. So the fear of calamity is based upon some emotional precedent from the past, real or illusory. Without risk, the future remains the past. No matter how miserable, it is secure.

But risk is the content of now, and without risk there is no now. The present moment, the immediate feeling, is gone, lost. (The exclusive concentration on breathing in yoga is a way of focusing upon the actual process of drawing in life; most people cannot do this without an accompanying, intrusive clutter of past-oriented thoughts.) Now can be a time of terror because *now* we are closest to ourselves, and we do not own ourselves.

It would appear that everything we do, we do now; but as adults, most of us actually do now only that which will gain us something in the future or reestablish something about the past. Such examples are infinite—but there is at least one that is not so obvious. Sexual pleasure, which certainly seems a *very* now experience. We engage in sex often because it proves something —a man's masculinity, a woman's desirability, a wife's debt to her husband, an aging man's illusion of prolonging youth, a conquest —and on and on. The sexual feeling itself, the implosion and explosion or orgasm, is very frequently only a by-product; sometimes it does not happen, and when it doesn't everybody gets depressed or rancorous or both. Because sex, too, has become abjectly utilitarian. It is a vehicle: a woman shrieks "I made it" —an accomplishment fed by an obsession that she must, *should* make it—while the male counters with "I made her make it." And both are happy, not with pure pleasure and feeling, but because they have successfully accomplished an exercise in the Judeo-Christian ethic: they have defined themselves through a piece of work; nose to the grindstone, ear to the ground, they have triumphed. Perhaps this is how we defuse our sexual anxiety —in the same way that we *work* at a marriage.

Real feeling has no goal: it is pure spontaneity, its end is the process itself. It is what a Zen master might call nothing—no *thing*. The orgasm; it is what it is. Uncontaminated.

This is in no way abstract; nothing about living is abstract unless we make it so in order to murder feeling. It is all very simple and has nothing to do with philosophical theories of time. The Zen Koan,[3] for instance, is absolutely and marvelously mad in its verbal silliness precisely to hammer home the point that if life is confronted intellectually—as Western man has done when he is not feeling the guilt of sin—it is not lived, that if life is considered as a set of problems, again it is not lived. If answers are sought to a non-problem . . . well, the conclusions of such a search are obvious.

We must turn to a particular experience of children as they relate to parents, in a context of ownership of life, limb, thought, and feeling—on their way to being collectivized. And I regard this as the root of all anxiety, of all sham, of all emotional disorder, of the loss of self. Children become disordered and grow chronologically into disordered adults trapped in time because their now has been stolen—a necessary theft if they are to be possessed. This is how it works: by nature there is nothing a child should or will feel wary about in relation to his own body, feelings, thoughts, and fantasies—unless he is *impressed that they are wrong or unacceptable* and begins to experience them somewhat along the lines of what Harry Stack Sullivan has called "not-me" [4]—a "me" that is forbidden expression by those people upon whom a child depends for nurture, love, and survival. But the implications of this are phenomenally far-reaching; the child is a living unit that receives sensory impressions from outside and from self-stimulation. The *whole* organism responds, and it always responds *now*. All these impressions and feelings occur now and at no other point in time. And when a parent impinges at this point in time, not only is the child's activity experienced as "wrong," *but so too is all of existence at that moment.* One does not exist: time itself must be repressed before any activity or thought that fills it. The anxiety is intense. Life stops, the present dies, and consequently we are not what we feel, we become detached from what we must not feel.

Consequently now has only one meaning: it is something to be avoided. It is the realm of honest, legitimate, real feeling. It is what we are, our identity; but we deny it and conform to

the wishes and dictates of others. This is why we have traditionally clung to the worlds of our parents—the only worlds we have
ever known—because we were not permitted consciously to forge
our own. What we were, or could have been at any given
moment, was seized. And that is why we are afraid of now: to
feel it, acknowledge it, is to be hopelessly cast adrift from the
world we have always known.

Reflection: We are sitting on the patio fronting a friend's
country house, drinking, talking. Sylvia, my friend's wife, is not
quite here. She is examining her three-year-old son, who is staring
dreamily, one hand down his shorts, playing with his penis.
When the hand pulsates against the cloth of the shorts like a
pumping heart, Sylvia is even more not here: she frowns, something angry in the eyes, teeth nibbling a lip. Finally she says
to me, assuming that I have been as entrenched in her world
as she:
    "I can't stand when he does that: I hate it. What can I do?"
    The great expert replies:
    "Don't look, Sylvia."
    But exactly what she cannot do is not look. She looks. Stares.
Is she turned on? Could there really be such a thing as penis
envy? Why not? We go to the moon these days.
    "Don't *look*?" she stage-whispers, then grabs the kid's elbow
and yanks—a yank so powerful he is lucky all that comes out of
his shorts is his hand.
    Now *he* looks. Stares at her, the little face so painfully con-
fused that for a moment he resembles a movie madman. He
looks for something in Sylvia's face: reason? explanation? But
now what she cannot do is look. She turns to no one, sips her
drink, abandons her perplexity, says:
    "Enough of *that* crap."

The confusion in the child's face: mark it well. It will leave
overt expression only after his mother does this to him enough
times so that he stops touching and playing with what belongs

to him. Then the confusion will be imprinted inside him, and whenever he wishes to examine his own property he will feel some form of anxiety—what form is irrelevant. That he should feel it at all is the nub of the tragedy. But what is most relevant is that the anxiety he will feel has less to do with sex than with the need to stop life on the spot; instead of feeling life he will lose time. The impulse of the moment, the sensation of now, is destroyed. So that whenever he feels "illicitly" sexual he will have to do something else—build a model airplane, take a shower, work, fight, get angry at something—all to avoid a *now anchored in total reality*. Now can be anything, not only a sexual moment; but no matter what it is, it is honest—and the destruction of it is an existential murder which becomes an existential suicide. The child will become not what he is but what the possessor wishes him to be; even more negatively, he will not become what the possessor does not wish him to be.

You can also see the full blast of ownership in adult reactions to thumb-suckers—children who, as some research is beginning to suggest, may be brighter, more imaginative, and ultimately more "successful" than their peers.[5] Adults are constantly dying to pluck that thumb out of the child's mouth. Though the thumb belongs to the child, and sucking it probably means that he can rely more upon his own living flesh than upon a rubber pacifier, thus becoming dependent upon himself—well, no matter, they want that thumb out of his mouth. The reasons may be dreadfully complex, but in simplest form it is a bullying act committed by people who cannot let someone else have himself, experience himself, be in touch with his own body. All those things that we are not, that we have lost, that if present make up an integrated human being, we envy. We cannot abide seeing them even in our own children.

Children sometimes behave like members of those cultures that we love to call "primitive"—like the masses of India, only one possible example. Watch an Indian peasant eating and it is often like watching your child. The hands touch the food, carry it to the mouth—and without in the least idealizing anything, there is in this action an obvious direct touch between person and environment. We have lost this almost absolutely, *not because of the fork*, but because of the weird mentality behind the fork. "Civilization" comforts us. So we foist off its most hollow trappings on our children.

Now, there is no doubt that the current generation is preoccupied with "returning" to nature, and if truth be told it has been instrumental in creating what few reforms we are experiencing in environmental antipollution measures and in detoxifying food. But true to form we have taken a young ninety-dollar-an-hour model, dressed her in tattered shorts, shoved a container of yogurt in her hand, goosed her across a television screen, and are busily selling her as a member of the "natural generation." And then there are the nudists who attempt to cavort with nature, yet it is on the darker side of bad form for a man to produce an erection, even though it is one of the possibilities of a penis. But, returning to the episode with my friend Sylvia, when a child is fondling and manipulating its genitals, the body is completely absorbed in feeling, while the faraway stare probably has something to do with an accompanying fantasy. Yet there is no utilitarian purpose here, there is no conscious "Hey, this is great!" or "I made it!" It simply *is*. Intense immediacy. Doing with myself what I will because it is my right. Whatever now is to a child, he is defining it for himself. And it is nobody's business but his own.

It is his own business, too, when he sits and thinks and fantasizes. He might even be working out some problem or conflict, manipulating nothing but his own coping processes. Then comes the familiar scene of the parent asking "What's wrong?" or "What are you thinking about?" The child has not asked for anything—but enter the mother or father, sometimes both in overwhelming duet, impinging, encroaching, implying that something wrong is going on. And the time-warp is upon us again, and we get the converse of Sylvia's prohibition. Now it's "idle hands are the devil's workshop." Now the child drives his fantasies deeper inside and they become as unacceptable to him as stroking his genitals, and it all leads to a subversion of honesty and openness, and an inability to entertain even the watered-down idea that now can be an intellectual concept.

Reflection: Three young women—

Gwen cannot masturbate, cannot have an orgasm in sexual intercourse, yet she is convinced that unless she masturbates she will never really enjoy making love. But she cannot. She lies in bed and lets her hand creep up her thigh, touches her vagina, and the anxiety comes. She feels something, stops, does not go on, begins to cry, feels that her body is not hers. Her hand performs a journey of ignorance: she tells me that she first heard the word *clitoris* at age twenty-one. She tells me that she still does not really know how she is "built." Her mother is convinced that a vagina is God's punishment.

Lucille can masturbate, but what she cannot do is think what she wishes to think. Every creative fantasy, every threat of self-discovery, leads to stomach pain. She cannot finish college because that is what she wants. She cannot play the violin because *she* wants to. So she eats and climbs close to 190 pounds, and eating is good not only because it fills her but because she can focus upon the amount she shouldn't eat. When she feels good, she immediately feels lonely. To be with herself is to feel totally isolated; to be with others is to look in on them while she is far away like a speck in a telescope reversed.

Mary hates her father because her mother hated her father, but Mary hardly knows her father because her mother divorced him when Mary was seven and he went away somewhere. He writes Mary a few times a year, but she never answers him because she hates him. When Mary was seven her mother told her that if the judge asked her to make a choice between mother and father, Mary was to choose mother. Mary can remember nothing before the age of seven; her father is obliterated. She has assumed until recently that no one remembers anything at all before seven. She has driven away, lost, seven years of her life. Seven whole years because she dare not remember that she may not have hated her father. Seven years lost: a Dachau of the spirit.

The ownership gets to be complete after a while—over body, thoughts, soul. Time is not our own; so our lives are not. To become de-possessed a person must be able to feel and think spontaneously, thus getting back at least some sense of what one is. Feeling alone is insufficient, since both feeling and thinking have been controlled; both are the lost content of time stolen. And here, I think, is where this generation strays badly, in their emphasis only on feeling. But this is natural since they perceive that their feelings have been crippled by intellectuality and circular words bereft of meaning and truth. Thus they feel that thinking and feeling are split off from each other (indeed, they can be) when in truth they are coordinated. This is why they have helped evolve therapies that are emphatic in their stress on feeling without (at least on the surface) intellectual content—and thus they cannot fully approximate the time destroyed.

I am not going to say more about this here—only to suggest for the moment the intensity of our children's search for their lost emotional life. We, of course, are pursuing our humanness in different ways—not by direct attack, but by an amazing variety of back doors. Opening one, we frustratedly discover still another.

6

The Masculine Role:
A Murder of the Self

We open back doors because we cannot rid ourselves, really rid ourselves, of the roles we play. And yet the roles stifle us; they are much more like blinders than masks, limiting our human vision. The damaged capacity for real emotional commitment has always been far more apparent in men than in women. A man's "commitments," his role, traditionally hang on the hook of broader social issues and upon work and productivity outside the home. Being the "breadwinner" has split men off from full participation in family life, thereby castrating a vital avenue to becoming human. This, I believe, is a bedrock issue in the resentment of wife and children, the home they represent, and the pursuit of extramarital sexuality as a way of feeling alive and finding some sort of identity. The resentment often, if not most of the time, simmers beneath the surface of awareness. And, since it is somewhat out of awareness, rationalizations for discontent splatter like misaimed buckshot: romance has gone, youth erodes into wrinkles, a myriad such reasons. What actually happens is that family becomes equated with the oppression inherent in the male role and it is almost easier in our society for a man to divorce his wife and abandon his children than to quit his job. His masculinity is thereby preserved. He has no need to question the pernicious role that he has swallowed whole, and so no need to discover himself.

Over the generations, men have changed outwardly far less than women—which is why women find them so intractable. It is worth repeating that men have uncritically accepted their social posture: the goal is to be a *man*—whatever that is. Failing this goal they feel like little boys: helpless, dependent, impotent. To achieve the social goal of *man* they struggle, compete, work to exhaustion usually for someone else. (A woman, after all, *does* work for her own even if she is "only" a wife and mother.) And decades of struggle and work entitle men to a number of rewards:

Heart attacks, hypertension, lung cancer, alienation from family, chronic fatigue, alcoholism, psychotic episodes called nervous breakdowns, profound depressions, all the Librium and Valium they can eat—and then the wait for death in a geriatric internment camp.

A upper-middle-class man can earn these fringe benefits in one job; a lower-middle-class man needs two. The arena is the economic structure: we have agreed that this is proper. Living is working and working has been a way of avoiding life. A way of dying.

I am very hard on men. They have for centuries proclaimed their insightfulness—but have rarely applied it to themselves. They adore each other's company or they avoid it flatly. Love it because of the sympathetic vibrations of mutual complaining; avoid it because they are too tired to compete. The epitome of the shallow male relationship is the bloodless liquid business lunch—a ritual during which neither party is interested in the other as a human being. They know this but collude in the game of pretending not to know.

They share the company of women (love aside) for more complicated reasons. They think that they do not have to compete, they can be waited upon, they can copulate aggressively to loose the anger that their daily roles may not permit and to save face if they have suffered some unmanning humiliation. Or they can be free to be impotent—which they dare not reveal during their working day. Although sexual impotence of any frequency gives men fits, paradoxically it may be the only way they can relax, avoid physical tension, ease out of the competitive arena without "blame." Quite simply, many men are too often too tired to get hard. At times they *need* softness, a halt to their aggressive displays.

Men have been raised to be performers. In a way it is all they know. Performance defines their identities: they must *do*, and whatever they *do* becomes a value, no matter how trivial. When they see freedom in others it is often an affront to them, and they stress duty and responsibility in a plainly hysterical way. The greatest reactionaries of all time have been men: they will deny the possibilities of their own personal freedom with a lunatic passion. They want all men to share the miseries of the burdens they refuse to relinquish. They seem to love their suffering, probably because, as Schopenhauer long ago hinted, they are so very good at it. *Any* victory is victory.

What the majority of men do all day is terrifying to contemplate. They support structures that destroy them. They run about like deprogrammed insects in jobs that by and large do nothing for anybody except to insure the cash flowing to the people on top. We call this maintaining the economy and participating in the freedom of democratic capitalism—the end point always being money, with plateaus of success or failure on the way up or down. Women, at least, can be mothers and so engage in life; but there might be futility in watching the life that one has nurtured become swallowed up in the maelstrom. If one recognizes it.

Men remain essentially cavemen, wielding briefcases instead of stone axes. They still live within the ethic of the primal horde. Each man waits to be knocked off: every company has a comer or two that one must watch—and when the comers arrive they must watch the newcomers. The system locks a man into perpetual tension, anxiety, and real fear, and there is no more effective way to keep a man in this position than to get him overextended so that he cannot bail out.

Do women really want to get involved in this? Do they understand this aspect of the "man's world"? Not on a conscious level —and therein lies an idealization of the most tragic kind.

Men are supposed to be assertive, self-starters (the term beloved of employment agencies)—the unintentional parody being the man in the pill ad who, with unflinching eye contact and outthrust jaw, convinces us that it is hard to stay on top. Sometimes he bites off more than he can chew and then his head aches and his stomach flames and he medicates himself—unless he feels *truly* sick. But overall he is as happy as a pig in shit: he is perfectly identified with his role. His way is correct.

The ad is a perfect illustration of the viciousness inherent in man's victimization of himself; his goal is the top, he must get there and stay there, and it is actually a good thing if he suffers physical and emotional stress in the process—*a stress that he must alleviate himself* or experience some variant of shame. The ad strikes a universal, mythic note, because we don't know what this pitchman does except dress neatly and make money. It suffices that he is on top. Of something, anything. Our hero. The best of us. The president of something. He has become what he was brought up to be. But there is no rest. He must fight and claw to stay there.

Of course the self-starter idea is a hoax, but it makes a man feel great while he is quickly swallowed up in some corporate structure where he is tossed a salary disproportionately low compared with what he accrues for others. He is also tossed an additional emotional bone by being called creative. But creative is precisely what he has been trained *not* to be. He has been trained to be a piece of machinery (self-starting is a reaction to a timing mechanism and nothing else) because a major ingredient of success is an apparent lack of feeling or the capacity not to show feeling—though it has an odd habit of creating tension, cardiac arrests, depressions, and maybe a trip to the shock-box doctor.

Doing has been confused, in many cases deliberately, with creativity—but it is really a substitute for creativity. (Psychotherapists like to consider themselves creative, but they actually are not. They are clever and generally well-meaning; they are performers with the creativity of *actors*, the best having a good sense of timing. It is the patients who are creative.) Men have been raised to *do*, are *supposed* to do, and doing can cripple a person because it is too often an escape from feeling, a flight from awareness. Doing is the true acting-out of our time: it prevents insight. But it is not called acting-out so long as someone places a stamp of social approval or value upon it. This partly explains why men are not, on the surface, as strongly affected by emotion as are women. They have been trained to flee it, fear it, scorn it.

Little boys are cooed over and very often become family prizes; immediately at birth they will pass their sisters on the preferment ladder. Yet many fathers hold back the physical affection they feel somehow freer to give their daughters. So boys receive most of their direct *warm* human contact from their mothers, while fathers get to be seen as somewhat detached, perhaps even cold, and the pattern of man as emotionally muted is put into operation. Later contact with father is quite often along lines of roughhousing, which is competitive and can even be scary if it constitutes the first real contact between father and son. Eventually the boy joins the Little League or something equally suitable where he is driven to desperation by adult coaches, forced to compete, and given the message that if he is injured he should not cry. Of course there is a Little League World Series, which brings the competition to fever pitch, and by the time they are age ten or twelve we have already separated the winners from the losers.

A logical result of this occurred recently when a boy was disqualified from the Soapbox Derby for doctoring his auto. The reaction of horror was ridiculous, and in some quarters insincere, because we all really know that in our society it's whether you win or lose, not how you play the game. You simply mustn't get *caught* at inventive cunning or "cheating." The boy with the soapbox car was merely working within the system; he will probably do very well. (And there have been rumors that the Little League champions of 1973 were older than the rules permit.) The early emphasis on competition cripples; the boy with the low self-esteem, the boy who must win, will find a way— and finding it he will lose his identity.

Now with girls pushing their way into the Little League, something fascinating is already unfolding. And it is sexual. A number of mothers are frantic, worried that boys will tag girls in the crotch or on the breasts, or that an errant ground ball will leap off the grass and knock out a tooth. Presumably such an injury will preclude marriage: what man will want a woman whose tooth has been crunched out on a baseball field?

And what will the girls do when they get hurt? Cry? This might trigger off the boys' crying response, natural in wounded children but unseemly in Hank Aarons and Mickey Mantles. Or will the girls swallow their tears and become little "men"?

What I am hinting at is this: the traditional view of women as not equipped to *do* anything "significant" (male) may be the false perception, the sexist posture, that will really help to liberate them. Because awareness and self-understanding can only occur if a person permits himself to be passive and receptive. To men passivity is a positive terror, and true receptivity is all but impossible since it implies a *taking in* of someone else's ideas, feelings, and thoughts. The competitive orientation teaches us to fight, debate, parry, thrust—but not to take in. Unless what we take in is some form of cold information that will gain for us something practical in the future.

Men are not on their way to freedom under their own fuel, because they repeat their stale cyclical patterns. To be free they must permit themselves to feel and fantasize. And certainly I don't think that women's freedom will result in joining the world of men as it is structured now—a horror show of sublimated murder. (Nor do I think that women will be any freer if they stick to their own kind, like segregated rows of boys and girls in parochial schools.) But if men can permit themselves to enter the world of feeling (traditionally the woman's domain), they may gain access to their softness and receptivity. What they risk is to come alive.

Reflection: Fred lost his editorial job in a huge publishing firm because he let two manuscripts slip by; they eventually made a lot of money. Fred was anyway too "literary" in his company: he still searches for a young Joyce or Faulkner. When he was fired, a comer took his place.

He tells me that when he gets home after his last day's work he wants to get blind drunk but can't. The house is quiet. His wife doesn't say much, sensitive enough to know that optimistic banter will irritate him. His infant daughter is asleep, his four-year-old son is just going to bed. There is something strange about the scene but he can't put his finger on it. Then he realizes that it is still light outside; he can't remember when they had all eaten supper together on a weekday. He tucks his son in bed, peeks in at his daughter, begins to wander around the house. Suddenly he is nauseous, runs to the bathroom, vomits, then sits on the edge of the bathtub. He thinks of mortgages, loans, bills, failure; dredges up more vomit, sweats.

That night he is sleepless. Some time toward dawn the baby

wakes, and his wife wakes to nurse. Fred tells her to wait, he will get the baby; and when he lifts her from the crib and touches his cheek to hers, he begins to cry. Back in bed his wife nurses and he lets his fingertips lay gently on the baby's head. Very quietly he continues to cry.

For the next few weeks he doesn't look for a new job; he stays in the house. Each morning he helps his son get ready for nursery school, eats breakfast with him, talks to him, sees that it will take time to get to know him. He gives his daughter supplementary bottles, observes what his wife does during the day, helps her. Some new knowledge begins to open before him, but he can't see it clearly yet; he panics a bit when he has to dip into his savings to pay a few bills. He plays with his children, shares the day with his wife. He feels happy. He feels that he is where he should be. Home, with his family.

He finds a low-key job with a small publisher and takes a sizable salary cut. He worries, but they make it. What is important now, vital even, is that he comes home early; sometimes he can take a three-day weekend. What he tells me finally is this: "Those weeks at home with my wife and kids—that's where I belong. I could never go back to the way it was. Never. Because the way it was was a corrosion. It was death. I never knew my family." He pauses, shakes his head. "And the worst part of it was that I thought I did."

Without design, without intention, Fred had abdicated fatherhood. He had never had an emotional involvement with his children; he had been absent. Knowing him, he would eventually have tossed a football around with his son, taken him places that we agree fathers should take sons. But there would have been no deep connection. He would have become a model for his son, but one who worked, worried, and competed, and, perhaps out of the need to model and imitate, the boy would feel that his father's role was the meaning of a man. And yet it would have been his mother who would truly raise him—and she would have patterned him more directly to the male role than his father ever could. This seems a paradox, but I will elaborate it a bit later.

Fred's plight was hardly unique, but his reaction to it was *very* unique. Most men in his position would brood, feel castrated and bitter, hit the gin or Valium bottle—*in relation to losing the job. Most* men would have distanced themselves from their families; a child's cry would be sandpaper rubbed over a wound. They would fall mute into a self-consuming depression—then eventually perhaps rally.

Why most men would do this is simple. The competition—work ethic again. He, man, is what he does, not what he is, and if his identity is so inextricably tied to what he does, then work must by definition be *the* cardinal value. Or else he is nothing. This belief is clearly seen in many mental hospitals where a target treatment goal is getting male patients back to work. Usually they get back too quickly and split open again, and this simply adds "evidence" to a diagnosis. But most work is spurious productivity, yet an agreed-upon criterion for "mental health." I have even heard a consulting psychiatrist suggest that a two-time job loser be sent to the dungeons of a state hospital because he had had his "chance" at "good" in- and outpatient treatment.

As far as I am concerned, the less emphasis on work the better. Because a patient who leaves work is trying to tell you that he is nauseatingly weary of his role, of competing, of trying to prove something. We won't allow him this respite, this insight even; we don't allow him to consolidate his feelings, make his choice. Probably we are envious of his ability to stop, afraid of his insight into his personal sham—which we fear may also be *our* sham. We send him back to work, and if he flubs it again and again we call him a borderline schizophrenic with a highly disturbed masculine self-image.

We despise such people for their capacity to drop out; we wish that *we* could. And if we wish it powerfully enough, our children will do it for us. If they do it by conscious decision they are malingerers, pariahs, hippies; if they do it without apparent conscious decision they are sick. Of course the anti-welfare contingents have a field day in this area: they want people to work. Work at *what* is not even an issue. For social dregs, *what* doesn't count.

I remember when I was just in training and asking people all sorts of silly and naive questions. I once interviewed a man who had turned down countless menial jobs. When I asked him why, he said very calmly, "Wouldn't you?" He was strikingly different from the men who drop out due to "physical" ailments that defy diagnosis or treatment, and collect their welfare, compensation, or social security checks. Bus drivers who complain of dizziness and split vision; waiters who have left- or right-sided weakness; and anyone can suffer crippling lower back pain. Men still must save face in order to justify any violation of their masculine image. The establishment hates them. Another example: I met a man who was so deeply disturbed emotionally, so out of it, that it was impossible for him to work on any job that required him to relate to a supervisor. Several pieces of supporting evidence were "overlooked" by a board of review that wished to deny his compensation claim. They wanted to call him a malingerer.

If men do not summon up the courage to extricate themselves from their roles, they will never be free. Men, as did Fred, need to reenter their homes instead of finding ways to get further away from them. They must allow themselves to be dependent, cared for, nurtured. But they never will as long as these real human needs are seen as weaknesses.

So if men are not what they *do*, if they are not their roles, what, then, *are* they?

They are bundles of unconscious forces who understand little about themselves. And because of this they are not yet fully human. Rigidly accepting their roles, they permit themselves no choice at all and often rise to the pinnacle of sublime blind idiocy. For instance: in April of 1974, legislation prohibiting discrimination against homosexuals was vociferously opposed by the New York City firemen and policemen, while the Roman Catholic archdiocese leaped on the bandwagon. The reasons *consciously* stated? Homosexuals in these positions would be detrimental to "morale" and "discipline." Maybe what everybody is really afraid of (note the word *discipline*) is the materializing of the following fantasy into an actual news story:

GRAB-ASS IN THE FIREHOUSE

New York City was completely burned last week when the city's firefighters failed to respond to alarms.

The fire commissioner attributed this massive failure of discipline to homosexuals who over the past few months have converted local firehouses into "hotbeds of perversions and orgies," and who have "got our good men involved by breaking their morale." The commissioner added that alarms throughout the city went unanswered due to a simultaneous orgy "which was obviously planned and timed to the second." He went on to say, "I don't know if any of your black or militant groups were behind it, but I know that homosexuals were."

It was also learned that police were ineffective during the great fire. A department official attributed this to "transvestite officers dressed as policewomen," but he declined to elaborate.

A spokesman for the Archdiocese of New York commented only that "we will abstain from any statements lest we be accused of an 'I-told-you-so' position."

I think that what men must do is face the possibility that much of what they are engaged in is a way of validating an illusion—the illusion that the ingredients of masculinity are clearly set forth in some divine recipe. *Men* must work. *Men* must be heterosexual and actively so. *Men* must assume prime financial responsibility in the family. *Men* have specific, approved occupations. Etcetera. Actually, men don't have to do any of these things. Yet they think they do, believe they do.

A woman may be burdened, sometimes overwhelmed to the point of rage and tears, by the responsibilities of raising children —but at least the work is real, it is not an illusion couched in socially approved clichés such as community-mindedness, economic stability, personal creativity, helping others, and all the rest of it. In truth, women have always lived more in touch with the realities of existence: we hear of earth mothers, never of earth fathers. They can know what it is like to feed a child with the nutriments of their own bodies, to deliver a child, to be reminded by their periods of their ability to create life—a *real* creation. But the so-called realities of men are very often the illusions themselves.

Collectively, men are a dangerously, violently, suicidal bunch. The need to be brave, have *macho*, has littered the battlefields of the world with men's own dead bodies, it has painted the streets with the blood of gang wars. Courage and toughness and heroism are the imposed fabric of a man's life even when he is in the cradle. A friend looks at my infant son and thinks he will be a professional football player; another predicts that he will be a heldentenor. The images appear different but they are essentially interchangeable: a heldentenor will sing Siegfried, who wielded a magic sword, who slew a dragon, who sings, *Fight with me or be my friend.*

And both images underline the inescapable point that almost all men are raised to perform. Is there any man who has not had a childhood hero? There is always someone to emulate, compete with, shoot at—and usually to fall short of and suffer defeat as a *man*.

> Reflection: Joey could run like the wind, throw a baseball like a cannon-shot, field shortstop like an angel. But he couldn't hit his way out of a wet Kleenex because he stood at the plate like a wound-up spring. Like the great Stan Musial —his hero. When the coach tells him that his batting stance is fine for Musial but unnatural for *him*, Joey says, *If I can't be Stan the Man I don't want to be anybody*. Indeed, he turned out not to be anybody.

So much of this explains sexism. Men have all but pulverized women—peers and daughters, but never mothers—into noncompetitive dust. They have done it via superior physical strength, biblical interpretations, restricted career opportunities, and transforming the penis into a thing that pierces a woman instead of caressing her. Men *need* noncompetitors; they value them more than anything else in the world. That is what a man wants his woman to be—and even if she only pretends to be submissive, well, that's all right with him. If he feels like making sexual war, needing some sort of victory to shore him up, he will search for a more resistant woman to "conquer." But at home he wants peace, compliance, a place to hang his helmet, spear, and shield, and get his feet bathed. At home he can always be a man—at least until recently.

These are some of the emotional trappings, but women will have to confront a few additional facts on their way to combating sexism now and vitiating it in the future. Sexism may be supported by men, but it begins and flowers in the relationship between mother and son while father is off somewhere turning his illusion into reality. (My point about bringing men into the home is important here. The father's assumption of a more active, consistent, and *feeling* position within the family helps to erode sexism at its core.) Women, mothers, perpetuate the illusion of traditional masculinity in their sons. In this sense men have sown the seeds of their own doom, solidified their own disastrous roles—because in keeping women children, women can only view men as powers upon whom they *must* lean for strength, prestige, comfort, and money. Women have not saved their sons from wars or even from sports that can maim and kill them. In Wagner's *Götterdämmerung*, Brünnhilde and Siegfried wake from their wedding night and she almost immediately says:

> *My beloved hero,*
> *if I held you back*
> *from new adventures*
> *what would my love be worth?*

Then with a quick twist into total narcissism:

> *If you wish to show me love,*
> *think only of yourself;*
> *remember your deeds;*
> *remember the raging fire*
> *you passed through fearlessly*
> *when it flamed around the rock!*

And shortly he marches off, naïevete in full bloom, to fires, floods, his destiny of death, and the twilight of the gods.

But this is the nub of it. In criticizing this passage, people have commented, "Ridiculous. Just a device to keep the plot moving by getting Siegfried on his way. A wife, a lover, would never send her man away so soon." Of course not. But a *mother* would. And mothers do. Through their sons they become heroes. They have never known any other way except to peer into the mirror of narcissism and see themselves revealed in an aura of power and glory. The Gold-Star mother (we never hear of a Gold-Star father) has gotten her son to engage in battlefield heroics *for* her, has gotten him to act out her hidden violence. And unconsciously she has murdered him.

So in this spirit I am going to make what could be construed as a profoundly unpopular statement: *Sexism is a product of the mother-son bond.* Every sexist attitude is in some way a derivative of this relationship, consciously or unwittingly—and we also have the common observation that a male chauvinist frequently treats his mother with a awe-inspiring respect. It seems a weird paradox, this simultaneous mother-worship and male chauvinism, until we resolve it with a crucial piece of knowledge. By persecuting and immobilizing women, by focusing his anger and superiority upon her, a sexist can preserve a harmonious relationship with the mother he still needs. And at the same time he continues to show her that she is the only worthy woman in his life.

Obviously this is an unpopular idea to both men and women. Women would probably rather believe that men perpetuate the "man's world." Men would probably rather believe that they are not the children, the victims, that they really are. Men and women have colluded in this together; they have compacted to despoil their humanity.

Men, of course, do not want heroines. What many men want is neatly symbolized by the plastic female dummies (vaginas included) sold via the sex papers: a woman who is inert, silent, and utterly unreal. It is the reality of women that terrifies men. When women speak, act, want, wish, demand—it is all a bit more than men want to cope with.

In short, the emergence of women as forceful, alive, independent human beings is the most threatening event in the collective history of men. And women must understand this. Not flaunt the knowledge or use it accusatorily (which would prove their ongoing hang-up with men), but simply understand it. Parity will come with blending, not belligerence.

On another front, men compete with their sons—comers in the familial corporation, intruders who threaten to take away mother's attention. Fathers and sons are often sibling rivals down deep; one shouldn't be lulled into the false belief that father is a man and son is a boy, period. They are both kids, fighting, the first blow struck by the elder. Also, a son is the only man with whom his father can successfully compete and win. At least until the son enters the greater arena, in which case he might leave the old man behind. But not in every way.

Reflection: Sam has done very well in life. By thirty he has a "good" wife, a child, climbs ahead in business, buys a house. He visits his parents, talks of the new house, and somehow gets involved in a Ping-Pong game with his father. After a couple of volleys Sam begins to warm up, cracking the ball back until his father is barely able to get a paddle on it. He keeps it up, flooded by a perverse glee, keeps smashing the ball back until his father throws down his paddle and snaps, "What the hell are you doing? You playing Ping-Pong or trying to kill me?" Sam gets upset, fumbles with a few words. He tells me that he took the question literally and couldn't come up with an answer. He has a bad night, round-eyed insomnia, wondering if much of what he has been doing all his life is connected to the metaphor of a murderous Ping-Pong game with his father. "I wanted to jam the ball down his throat." And then an apparent *non sequitur*, but no *non sequitur* at all: "My house is twice as big as his."

The nightmarish repetition of this pattern tempts one to wonder if it isn't in some way genetic, a web of fate, spun in the core of a collective unconscious. It seems that men have always been this way and always will be. Work, do, compete. Once it was necessary, when men had to kill animals in order to eat and beat off hungrier invaders with clubs and spears. This was the business of actual survival, of life itself. But now it is weird, because at first glance this desperate competition, this winning, fighting, seems so much in the service of acquiring luxuries, possessions, of getting a house "twice as big" as somebody else's.

Something very strange has happened in man's evolution from the necessity of sheer animal survival. The struggle for survival is now an *emotional* necessity since actual life survival is no longer an issue except in starving and still primitive cultures and ghettos. In this context I think that we are in a greater state of flux—some would say chaos—than in any other time in our past. And there is no reason to predict that we will stabilize —at least in the near future. Those who have solved problems of basic needs and now have only an emotional need to survive exist in a world with those who still wear rags and forage for a crust. The emotional needs have been converted to ideology, particularly in America.

For instance, our participation in the Vietnam war was heavily propagandized along ideological lines of stemming Communist expansion and all that that implies. The Vietcong, however, despite the philosophy of Ho, were considering more basic issues of survival rooted in the need for food and territory. Ideology was a completely secondary matter; it was a nonaffordable luxury.

The fact seems to be that men require an enemy, a competitor, and the more they refuse to deal with their inner forces, their aggression, violence, and fear, the more they will set up external situations that *appear* actually to threaten their physical existence. Men do not, as a rule, search inwardly. Until they do so, their potential awareness will remain anesthetized by the propensity to act—activity always being mistaken for dynamism and achievement.

Murderers are condemned; the movement is on to reinstitute death penalties for society's more expressive killers. Our civilized social outlet for murder is the competitive arena of achievement and success. That is how we channel raw aggression, perpetuate the channel, insist on it, and thereby break men who either refuse to engage or who lose in the engagement. The unbounded violence of it all is seen especially in power politics, where any means to an end are justified so long as the more sordid and destructive elements are hidden from public view. We have agreed to tuck our murderous instincts behind facades.

Perhaps the real lesson of Watergate is that a violently competitive, power-oriented President did not understand the concept of overkill, did not understand that the "sacred" precincts of the White House were not an appropriate field for the street brawls and paranoia of the gutter. In going too far to solidify his position —too far because at root he panicked—he blew the ball game. Friends became enemies, called him shabby, shoddy, immoral. His inability to hide his belligerence, his need to win the same battle repeatedly—his *utter obviousness*—caused us to want to punish him. He would not let us cherish the illusion; he revealed to us what we wish to keep invisible. And it doesn't matter at all whether he was guilty or innocent. His *style* was his crime. As was Oscar Wilde's. Wilde, who was punished not for his homosexuality, but for its exposure in public.

Most of the activities of men are perversions of human aggression, yet in some odd way stepping-stones to the future, a transition of pain and despair, a world trembling under the rule of men who are still unaware of their dependency and real motives. I don't think that women are much like this; at least they do not have a history of collectively agreed-upon aggressive pursuits—unless we can call their age-old support of "male" activities a form of vicarious aggression. Of course, the question is, Will women behave differently from men when they come to solidify their social, political, and economic power bases? Then perhaps we can solve the riddle of individual differences for once and for all.

But the current fact now remains that men and women handle their aggression quite differently. Women, I believe, are incapable of making the following equation of power and sexuality:

George competes against a young co-worker for the design of a multimillion-dollar shopping center. At a board meeting he is told that his plan is accepted—and the tension begins to mount. His plan will be a prototype for at least a dozen more such centers; banks are bidding for the privilege of financing the project; his firm has become the darling of the stock-brokers; his bonus will reach high into five figures. George feels like a balloon slowly filling, almost euphoric, speechless as he sits at the polished oak table bathed in the smiles of his superiors. And then? And then George has an orgasm.

A knotty problem for students of the future.

7

Farewell to Adam's Rib?

In the roots of our weird male superstructure hides the woman, wielding her incalculable covert power. In the past she earned respect only through motherhood. Marriage was an expectation; but motherhood was the power site. A man may beat his wife even though she is the mother of his children. But he may never beat his *own* mother.

Women, mothers, like the nuns at Saint Catherine's, are obviously powerful molders of their children. But most important, their children—particularly male children—become the actors of their unconscious scripts. I don't really blame Gold-Star mothers: sending their sons off to die was secondary to the wish to be aggressive, assertive—to be *somebody*. Not to be a man, but to have his prerogatives even though they might be suicidal. They wanted to grow up, to be human, but they could not do it with the direct force of their own wills.

Women, as I mentioned before in passing, have not been kept subservient because they are inferior—though there is much lip service to that effect. (Where are the female Bachs, Picassos, Jeffersons? And similar rubbish.) They have been kept children,

children being the single group of human beings who have absolutely no rights, no permission to grow in their own ways and claim the privilege of self-ownership. To insure that a chronological adult remain a child you must constantly criticize, limit curiosity, define a preordained role and code of behavior —and continue to cripple any move toward autonomy and free choice. (Rousseau: "One captures volition itself.") As soon as the crippling process is accomplished within the basic family, society immediately reinforces it by hammering down the lid on adult opportunity.

Women have been kept obedient and possessed children in countless ways, especially sexually. Actually, following the myth of the pure, sugar-and-spice, ignorant child, the traditional norm for women has been asexuality. They have been expected to comply with marital sexual demands, but not to enjoy sex, *never* to initiate it—in short, to be as ignorant and unfeeling about their sexuality and genitals as it is humanly possible to be. Whatever odd, involuted ideas have been fostered by Freudians concerning female sexuality, Freud made one single, vital truth known to a hostile, disbelieving society: "nice" women, not just promiscuous tramps, were intensely sexual animals and that repressions of their normal sexual feelings and wishes resulted in neuroses of the most bizarre kinds.

Even more importantly, women have been raised to view themselves as damaged, inferior human beings, and this has been reflected in clothing, makeup, "feminine" products. Even so short a time as ten to fifteen years ago, a woman unquestioningly wore a bra, often a girdle that had metal clips to hold up stockings, spiked heels—refuse of the age of elaborate boned corsetry and cagelike hoop skirts. While such nonsense has been seen as a way of being sexy for men, it is really a kind of harness or surgical brace which suggests that the female body is intrinsically defective, warped. In the same way, padded breasts and hips are thinly disguised prosthetic devices—like artificial legs. Cosmetic nose jobs, siliconed breasts, tooth crowns and implants, face liftings, were invented for women; so were dipilatories and underarm deodorants. And, later, deodorants for genitals and feet. Also the billion-dollar cosmetic industry. Now while you can say that much of this weirdness is aimed at titillating men—which it is, and frighteningly so—there is a far more crucial point behind it all. Namely, that a woman is a piece of genetically defective machinery, her body needs reforming and constant servicing lest it fall apart. And she stinks. In certain religious sects she still cannot touch a plant or have sexual contact while menstruating. And, lastly, she is made to fear her own female organs: there is more than a slight touch of hysteria in the incessant magazine articles about breast cancer, ovarian cancer, hysterectomies, whatever. So a woman is not only defective and smelly, she is always on the verge of death *because* she is a woman.

How a woman can emerge from this mess with even a semblance of self-esteem is a major miracle of human resilience. While I will always maintain that Freud, at least in theory, was a pioneer women's libber, psychoanalysis was relatively blind to these social pressures, this view of woman as defective. So the idea of penis envy was developed to explain women's feelings of inferiority—and here Freud reverted to the male chauvinism of his Victorian era. For example, the hypothesis that the clitoris is a vestigial penis is no more than the biblical Adam's rib theory—that Eve was created from a part of Adam—a vestigial idea in itself. There may well be such a thing as penis envy—but this is an artifact of living in a society partly structured on possession as an absolute, with the concomitant idea that one must envy anything that one does not have, be it a penis, a womb, or a subscription to the Metropolitan Opera. Certainly women have envied *man* for his "intact" and disease-free body, for his apparent freedom to enjoy sex and social opportunity. If legless, I am always going to envy a person who can walk even if my "adjustment" looks marvelous and I am kind to my physical therapist. Also, we have turned the natural process of childbirth and motherhood into a institution of enslavement so that not only can a woman come to despise motherhood, and by extrapolation her family, but she has also another reason to envy the "freedom" of men.

In the past—and we are only making initial inroads today —woman has been able to live with herself by remaining naive or repressed. She *had* to accept this role as ordained by God. Without this acceptance, she could not live at all. In order *not* to feel like a degraded slave, she has pretended not to be one, to accept her role—except for those incredible women who have deviated such as George Sand or Madame Bovary—or she has become mad with a frightening emotional honesty that could not be blinded to the vicious game. Sexual drives were stifled to justify the "truth" of social norms; intellectual activity was repudiated; matters of the real world became the province of men. In essence, all forms of curiosity were expunged or pushed deep into the depths of the unconscious. And thus we had robots, not only children but children who appeared vaguely brain-damaged. It used to be called "flightiness." Psychiatry has labeled it "emotional lability"—the swing between all sorts of buried emotions that pop through the fake social crust of what a woman *should* behave like.

Over the aeons, the centuries, with man's decreasing need of physical strength, women have achieved potential parity via the innate strength of their emotions and the innate equality of their brains. It is these two factors that have been suppressed, blocked—and then excoriated as inferior by the very society that crippled them. (I once heard the sicknening story of a blue-eyed blond Jew in a Nazi extermination camp who had his eyes gouged out and his hair burned away, thus proving that physiologically he was obviously not an Aryan.)

Sexually stupid and passive, a woman cannot be a threat

to a man's virility: even if he is the word's worst lover, how would a naive woman know? It may be the deeper intense attraction of man to woman that causes him to cut the pull of the magnetic field. For every Emma Bovary there has been a Werther, for every Violetta an Alfredo—giving up everything in society for love and passion. And of course there is the power that a woman has as a mother—and men want to dominate their women as they could not dominate their mothers.

Reflection: I, of course, was brought up in that emotionally crooked generation where "nice" girls never even petted below the waist. Consequently we never made love to the girls who were "not nice" because they hung out in sewers, whereas our territorial imperatives resided in ice cream parlors. At seventeen, Charlie got turned onto Joan who suddenly sat on his lap. They spent six solid summer weeks necking on her stoop until she broke it off. He was miserable and cried whenever we fed the jukebox a nickel for a love song. I don't know why he didn't know what *we* all knew—or maybe he did. Joan got plainly frustrated, then bored to take the edge off the frustration. Joan was not "not nice," but she wanted something more. Charlie either didn't know it or was too scared to know it. We, the boys, were poisoned, too, and we would live with a warped view of what a girl was. We still look for the "bad" girls.

Of course this is changing, and simultaneous with women's attempts to free themselves from traditional repressive roles is the growing trend to underline—in some quarters to glorify—the natural functions and capabilities that make woman unique, particularly around motherhood. There is La Leche (literally meaning "milk") which urges breast-feeding—but probably far beyond the time that a baby is interested in the breast. And there is the explosive interest in "natural" childbirth, exemplified by the Lamaze method. Lamaze training is excellent: it involves the husband, it imparts physiological knowledge. But there is a major caveat: it works when it works, that is, when the process of birth is smooth, uncomplicated. And it disdains pain. There is pain in childbirth, and one cannot pretend that it can be completely controlled—and while most Lamaze instruction is given by women, the pretense of utter control, no pain, is at root a sexist idea. I have seen many women who "broke" in the labor room end up lacerating themselves as failures. Only a short time ago a woman had to track down a physician and a hospital that permitted "natural" childbirth. Now, in our uniquely American way, it is the status symbol of the young, liberated middle class.

Reflection: My wife did not make it "naturally" the first time, but she is going to make it now—second children are easier, and there is excitement in the labor room. I am in my crumpled whites, and the midwives are there, urging, and we are holding her while she pushes. It is going like clockwork, a perfect synchrony of contractions and dilitations. It is, by Christ, natural. Then she rests for a moment, and one of the midwives jerks her thumb toward the next room, says: "What about her? *She* okay?" The answer is curt, disdainful: "Doped up like a zombie. She don't need *us*, honey." Another contraction, more pushing. "Lots of head there, honey; get the doctor." He comes, looks, smiles—with a courtly gesture waves me toward the door, says: "Shall we go?" They lift her to a stretcher, wheel her out, and we pause to let the zombie next door precede us into one of the two delivery rooms. I look at her face; her eyes look at me but I am sure they don't see anything. Maybe she wants it that way? Has to have it that way? Her obstetrician wants it for convenience? I don't know. But she is so quiet, so alone. My wife is breathing hard, flushed scarlet, yelping at times. I keep looking at the other woman, wheeled silently into the room then left there completely alone—as if she has just been gotten rid of. We enter our room and the delivery begins, and in the mirror above the table I see the head of the person who is going to be my son—coming, coming. The room is unbelievable: a college fieldhouse near the end of a winning basketball game. Home team a cinch; scoring baskets by the gross. There is cheering, yelling, applause, and I see that the room is jammed. A medical student lopes in to watch. A crowd. Then there is a possible complication and I must leave for a moment. The woman is still alone in the next room; the doctor is drinking coffee and talking with a resident. It is so much *his* ball game that I am annoyed; the woman lies there, without husband, midwives, nurses. Maybe in her stupor she doesn't feel alone. But it makes me sad. Then cheering resumes, I am yelled in, and in a minute my son is there and I am high and he seems to stare at his mother which gets me even higher. The anesthesiologist gives me her stainless steel revolving stool—a prize, she says, for a natural birth. The decibel level diminishes and I leave while my wife chats and they prepare to wheel her to her room. Outside the other woman's doctor yawns, walks slowly into the delivery room, and I know there will be no fun in that room, only a businesslike procedure. She will get no prize. She has not made the grade. The loneliness of that room almost chills me.

I hope that this is not the way the future points. I hope the "new" woman will not stare down her nose at the sisters who find it frightening to change, who are so locked into the past, the learned role, that the anxiety of change all but overwhelms them.

Now I am going to be impressionistic, make a collage of ideas, feelings, reflections about women and where I think they are, where they are going. Impressionistic is about the best I can be; I am not a woman, and women must find their own way, picking and choosing the best ideas they can, not being seduced by any theoretician or activist simply *because* she is a woman. There may be some ideas here, at least some feelings by a man who doesn't consider himself an MCP or a sexist—at least consciously. A man who also doesn't consider Ashley Montagu's belief that women are "naturally" superior as worth much of a damn. Here, in part, is how I have seen the human being called woman; reacted to her; thought about her; experienced her in personal life and in psychotherapy; reacted to others' feelings and thoughts about her.

I have never thought of women as inferior, not because of a precocious development of logic, a transfiguring experience, or a program of research; to me, women were never inferior because I was raised by a matriarch who herself was raised by a matriarch. She was the source of all power and strength and fantasies, and although she possessed me utterly, without her I could not have dreamed, could not have been a romantic, could not have sought my Isolde, could not have sung my *Parsifal*. Could not have written my books, nor gone off on incredible flights, nor approached my patients with imagination, nor understood the incredible longings and possibilities of all of us. Nor felt the pain and despair of living in mundanity, of fantasies failing, of being eaten at by the practicalities of life, of no longer being adulated as the W*ünderkind*. Destructive? Perhaps. But what was destructive I can try to alter; the other things one cannot buy, cannot acquire. Building; tearing down. They are the handmaidens of existence.

I wouldn't make a very good male chauvinist pig.

In elementary school it was a woman who became interested in the fantasies I began to put on paper. In high school a woman plucked me out of mediocrity and absorbed me in books and the theater. In college it was a woman who taught me enough Spanish to translate a novel by Unamuno; another taught me the glories of seventeenth-century English poetry; another revealed the essence of literary criticism; and still another worked with me on a very bad first novel to the point where it was almost published. One summer at the Breadloaf Writers Conference, it was a woman whose deft, simple suggestion made a story publishable. My first editor was a woman, and my literary agents are women who have stuck by me for seventeen years and whose wisdom I accept without reservation.

All my letters of recommendation to graduate school were written by women—and it was a woman, my wife, who encouraged me to enter psychology and who supported me financially and emotionally. Emotionally beyond anyone's call of duty. And it was our girl child who made me realize that I could be a parent.

The majority of my most brilliant, feeling, and intuitive students and supervisees have been women.

It just doesn't seem that I would make a very good male chauvinist pig. Or I could deny everything I have just written —and then I would make a very good one indeed.

The trap of motherhood. It pins a woman immutably to her past role and prevents her from developing her full human potentiality. It is thankless idiot-work, a chore, a hassle, oppressive.

And it is also denigrated because of fear, an inability to give (and sometimes take), and the web of intellectualizations built to justify avoiding it is conscious or unconscious fakery. It is close to impossible to find a woman who will flatly state that she does not want a child simply because she does not want one. Some defensive rationalization is always forthcoming. ("Howard and I kept moving around the country because he kept changing jobs, and I didn't want to shuttle a child from one school to another because I know how damaging that can be, and by the time we finally settled down I was over thirty-five and I was afraid I'd have a mongoloid.") Of course, social pressure partly forces the rationalizations; but do some women also feel that they have not fulfilled some biological destiny?

The inability for a woman to see that another human life, a child, can be an enrichment rather than a trap has to be the product of emotional strangulation and a reflection of a damaged childhood. She cannot conceive either that a child is a person or that it can give. She sees herself as giver, and the idea of such responsibility becomes overwhelming.

The attack on motherhood per se is far off the target. What deserves attack, and then radical change, are the socially bred destructive *responses* to motherhood: children have been extensions of selves, vicarious objects, trinkets to enhance narcissism, competitors, products ground out to please and placate parents and husbands and religious dogma. And very often these motives lead to a mother's feeling that her child is not really her child at all. Obedience to these pressures without choice is merely another piece of evidence of how childlike women have been kept.

Motherhood is not a trap; it is what it is. The trap has been built around it by disordered perceptions. To proclaim that motherhood as a state is a trap is tantamount to maintaining that abortion is "bad"—the commonality being that individual lives are adjudged to be less important than the "moral" concept. Like so: If my country is right whether it is right or wrong, and I do not choose to die for it, then I am wrong even though I may be right. This is not only sophistry, it is intellectual, moral, and emotional fascism. And I should hate to see women fall victim to it.

Actually the power of motherhood is intrinsic—just in terms of the incredibly long time children must depend upon mothers for nurture and learning to be human. (And there is massive evidence that primitive and even some advanced cultures were structured upon matriarchy.[1]) Freud and his followers focused primarily on the role of the father: psychoanalysis rested on the cornerstone of the Oedipal complex and one needed the concept of a powerful dominating father to carry the theory through. Naturally this was a dazzling reflection of the sexist Victorian society; but all the while there existed a subtle matriarchy, in which the role of the man was breadwinner and worker —like bees in a hive. One need only read Freud's letters to Martha Bernays,[2] and sympathetically suffer the pains of their almost interminable engagement, to realize the extent to which a man

felt he must financially and socially provide for a woman in
those days. What all men wanted were queenly mothers who
would care for them, attend to them.

The extreme underlying power of motherhood has been
"rediscovered"—but in a rather sad context. I mean the recent
heavy emphasis on the mother's unconscious role in abetting
schizophrenia; but this has also led to the converse realization
of the mother's power in raising emotionally sound children. In
essence, a child is brought up mainly via maternal rules of
conduct: a child must or must not do what the mother desires,
and its customary punishment for not toeing the line is the
withdrawal of love—in a child's world the most powerful weapon
imaginable. Unlike men, women have used the core family as
a power base, and, rich or poor, they could maintain the power
even if they appeared to be martyrs, victims of exploitation,
sexual objects.

And here is where many, if not most, women have missed a
crucial point. A man does not have to marry for sex. It is an
old wives' tale perpetuated mainly by women themselves, and it
has obscured much of women's real value. They have transferred
their power and importance to their genitals; this has resulted
from a misreading of men's basic desires and from stories told
by their mothers. It seems to me that most women have never
asked *why* certain men want to marry them. Sex is not the major
reason; rather it is the hope of reuniting with a mother and the
expectation of being taken care of unconditionally. A man
marries a woman from whom he can gain strength.

It is a fantastic power that a woman has. And as women come
more and more to enter the larger, extrafamily world, their
power will wane. It is waning now, which is one reason for the
erosion of the nuclear family: the cement, the binding force, is
loosening. Yet someone must raise children in order to free
mothers—relatives, nurses, day-care staffs. That person will
exercise the power, become in some way the "real" mother, and

the deep, unspoken, emotional bond between child and natural mother will be damaged. Or, less pessimistically, weakened. How this eventually works out we can only wait and see, but I have the feeling that such children will be strangers to their mothers; an unconscious mutual emotional attunement will be missing between them. Nightmarishly, all this sounds like the reincarnation of the upper-class aspects of the British Victorian era when nannies were the prime maternal figures—and that was a sexist society of the highest order, dominated, ironically, by a queen. Superficially it appears to work in societies that attempt to raise children via ideology—China, Russia, the *kibbutzim* of Israel. Superficially, because you cannot *really* nurture a human being with the milk of ideology. It may not work at all in a fragmented society such as ours, where stability is wobbly and the rule books of conduct are being immolated.

There is going to be a price for this "freedom," for opening the jail cells of motherhood. We must wait to see what this price will be.

Possibly, quite likely in fact, a woman cannot have it both ways: a full-time mother and a full-time explorer of other human potentialities that lie outside the family circle—although these value-laden potentialities may well be intrinsically worthless, a dumb show of society. Many women believe this and they —not ignorant, hedonistic, lower-class, impulsive sluts—have been the prime movers behind the new abortion laws, laws which are again under fire. And while these new laws are crucial for those women who feel that they do not want children, *and so should not have them,* these liberating laws raise an issue which has great human and legal implications for the future. By their own growing insistence, women want fathers to assume a far more active role in child-raising; and if a father is to be active he must be active all the way, and this implies equal voice. Here I follow the point made by Jonathan Weiss, a writer and lawyer deeply involved in legal protection for minority groups and the poor. Weiss advocates the establishment of a law giving the husband of a pregnant woman the right to veto an abortion if he agrees to assume all subsequent responsibility for the child. Of course, this implies a profound conflict between a man and woman which might well result in a broken relationship, or be the manifestation of an already damaged relationship. But the point is far-reaching and unavoidable: a woman is the biological carrier of the child, but this does not obviate the fact that a father, through his sperm and perhaps his sentiments, is half the process. The child is also *his*.

Yet I think that before we arrive at such possibilities we must first insure that the new abortion laws are safeguarded and vigilantly protected—not because of huge concepts such as cosmic overpopulation, but simply because they are necessary to prevent births that are not wanted. Children who are not wanted become warped, at times destroyed; so, too, do the mothers who do not want them. And I doubt that any antiabortion groups can support an argument in favor of such an outcome—though they try. They do maintain that abortion is murder and that the fetus has the right to life. But an unwanted child does not live, it merely exists, becoming the object of neglect, hatred, rage, and in some cases of *literal* murder. (That a Catholic mother can demonstrate against abortion under the banner of "the right to life" while letting her son plunge into the maw of Vietnam seems one of the more miraculous mysteries of our time. Except that death is not the issue.)

I think that all these right-to-lifers are violently enraged at any idea that a woman might have an essential right to call her body her own. Because we must remember that women have been kept infantilized by splitting them off from any control of their adult rights, particularly their sexual functioning. (It is their children who become sexual for them.) And the argument is always the same: women who abort are not intelligent, conscious beings but sluts who want *pleasure* without responsibility.

That is the core and it will always be so, because without a conviction that life entails suffering there can be no religion. Women must not take sexual pleasure, and if they do so they must take the consequences and pay the piper. The consequences are unwanted pregnancies, and their products are bastards who must also suffer. Yet this is called responsibility—which consigns mother and child to a slow inexorable process of living death.

Reflection: It is the spring of 1954 and a teen-age girl emerges from a bus into a large town in New Jersey that she has never heard of. She is nervous, finds the doctor she is looking for, and is immediately calmed when she speaks with him. He is almost completely gray, ruddy, relaxed, paternal. He tells her his frank feeling about abortion: it is advisable only for those women who are sure that they could not provide a good life for their child. Does she have any second thoughts? She does not. How can she? She is seventeen and cannot yet provide for herself. He discreetly asks for his fee. Eleven hundred dollars. As she must know, there are police that must be paid off so that he may continue his work. She is prepped by a nurse who hurries her, and then the doctor begins to hurry as well. She becomes nervous again; the atmosphere is very businesslike and somewhat hard. There will be only a local anesthesia since the doctor has no postoperative facilities, and her nervousness increases. She *is* having second thoughts, but she goes through with it and returns to a girl friend's house; her parents think she is away, spending an ordinary weekend there. She feels rotten, she hurts; she drinks a cup of tea with her friend, takes a pill the doctor gave her, and goes to sleep. Later that week her obituary appears in her hometown newspaper. But it doesn't mention anything about the embolism.

In the summer of the same year a black hooker is lying on her bed in Harlem, waiting for her pimp who has beaten the hell out of her for getting pregnant. She is waiting for him to return with a friend who works miracles with equipment not even made for the job, profit being the mother of invention.

The pimp comes back with the friend who wants five hundred which the pimp gives him, snapping at the girl that he'll get it out of her ass. The friend asks if she'll do it straight and she says, "Shit no, I'm a spade but I ain't crazy," so he just happens to have some H which is not included in the five hundred and she shouldn't worry about getting a habit from one medicinal fix—that is, if she hasn't got a habit already. Which she hasn't, at least not a smack habit. He shoots her up, she doesn't look at what he brings out of his briefcase which, like his shoes, is made of shiny tan dude alligator.

No obituary appears anywhere. There was so much blood that the cop who checked her out had the fantasy that she was worked over by a gang of Hell's Angels.

While the abortion laws must be protected, a very dangerous law has been passed in a number of states. This is the law that can convict an alleged rapist solely upon the testimony of the woman involved. Rape is a hideous crime; it is a crime specifically related to the legal recognition that women are biologically different from men. The rape of a male is not called rape; it is called assault. But have all women who claim to have been raped indeed been raped? This is a question of awareness. Women who are in touch with their sexual wishes and feelings, who achieve sexual satisfaction, who know when they are flirting—these women know when they've been raped. But many women are not in touch with their sexuality, do not consider themselves flirtatious or provocative—yet they may behave provocatively without awareness, always afraid of consciously initiating any sexual encounter. Any attempt at sexual intercourse may be perceived by such women as an attempted rape. Policemen, as well as psychologists, know this very well; and they know, too, that many true rapes are not reported because certain women are not sure what they might have done to provoke them. And they also know about the myth of the ubiquitous rapist who is huge, invariably black, and who carries a small armory of weapons. (I am not going to deal with those women who consciously accuse a man falsely.)

While such a rape law—no witness required—appeals to a *broad* feminist point of view, I cannot help but feel that it is part of a growing reaction to the "new sexuality." Because this law has to generate a hundred second thoughts in any man when he approaches a woman or accepts the approaches of a woman. It would be lovely to say that "good vibes" between a man and woman will carry the day; but it is a naive belief. Many men who give off "good vibes" have turned out to be rapist-murderers, and many women who give off "good vibes" have made false accusations.

The new law will create a new fear, a new anxiety, which might not only poison sexual contact but in some cases the possibility for a real relationship. It is an establishment law that tells me one essential thing: it is safer to consign sex to the marriage bed. All you risk there is the possibility of a broken relationship if it doesn't work out. If the divorce laws are reverted to adultery as the only grounds for separation, we will be back in the trap.

Women must not lose sight of a powerful fact: laws are still made primarily by men who as yet have no really clear picture of the power of their female constituency. Why would men approve a law that appears so dangerous to themselves? A question to answer the question: why did Italian lawmakers—who have never included a woman—keep in effect statutes forbidding divorce, and why do they continue to fight off more enlightened legislation? Could it be possible that men do not want to lose their mother-wives in the wake of sexual freedom?

What women *must* do is examine in minute detail every piece of legislation that seems exclusively in their favor, legislation that ostensibly puts a dent in male chauvinist pigdom. If the war against sexism is waged by hysterical troops, this examination will never be made. The catch in all of it will be the subtle construction of reaction—brick by brick until we are all walled in. Once out, let's stay out.

As the nuclear family erodes, so, too, does marriage as we have always known it, and I think that while many people are frightened by marital dissolution, it is a good thing, this dissolution of marriage as we have perpetuated and institutionalized it and tried to make it operate on a structure of idiotic symbols and fake obligations. We have taken such a simple thing as a relationship between a woman and a man and run it on shoals of irrelevancies such as religious supervision and economic necessity. Irrelevancies which have become far from irrelevant as they have been reinforced by time and surrender. We have made marriage, like religion, so restrictive and burdensome that all fun has been drained from it. Heavy stuff: the Catholics made it a sacrament, adultery is still punished by one or another form of stoning (though I have never heard of a husband being stoned). This heaviness, seriousness, solemnity: it was all built to keep the woman sexually dormant. We even have precedent: Eve, not Adam, was the one with the hot pants—which is undoubtedly why female genitals are dirty. Why couldn't the authors of the Old Testament just let Eve and Adam play, eat fruit, and make friends with the snake? With *that* kind of scriptural precedent we might have had a tradition of happy, free marriages where penises and vaginas, men and women, shared parity. Where questions of power and inferiority would not even have been considered. Well, it was all planned—the end of the story, that is—when the Hemingway of the scriptures, whoever he was, plucked the rib out of Adam and made of it a woman. But everyone *really* knows that Adam came from Eve. Even my small son knows that he came from his mother. The only males who give birth, as far as I know, are sea horses.

I forgot God in all of this. But then—why not? He has been accused of just about every absurdity in the history of the world.

Eating lunch one afternoon, I heard this from the next table: "You don't have to understand the *black* woman. She's been oppressed because she's a woman. Blackness has nothing to do with it."

She was somewhere in her mid-twenties, talkative, tense, middle class, and very white. Paraphrasing a line by Mel Brooks, I got such a headache I had to put out my cigarette.

Blackness has nothing to do with it. Except that black women have been raped and plundered and forced to clean our houses and carry shit off hospital wards, kept in servitude and ignorance by whites—including white women. They have raised their children not with optimism but with the goals of avoidance: hopefully their children would not become junkies, criminals, or die in the streets. No chance for even the minimal happiness of motherhood (motherhood, the white woman's trap). No real chance of a relationship with a man because the man washed cars and bussed dishes and also carried shit off hospital wards, and finally took off somewhere in hopes of avoiding a total spiritual death. Blackness has nothing to do with it. Because the woman at the next table, bottle-blond and martinied, could not comprehend it at all. She had never been a millionth of the way there.

All "movements," strong or weak, unified or fragmented, contain seeds of tyranny, and feminism is no exception. Specifically I mean attitudes toward homosexuality, which in itself is saturated with tyrannies of all sorts. In certain circles there exists the idea—a demand, really—that if a woman is to be truly involved with her sisters then she must (imperatives again) experience her femininity via sexual contact with another woman. Thus becoming more human. On one level, this is the position of the *insecure* homosexual seeking to normalize behavior that she anxiously suspects is "deviant" or wrong. On another level, the demand perpetuates the idea that women are children who must obey the wisdom of their more knowledgeable, experienced elders—to do the right thing, to please, obey, to be a good girl.

A woman, like a man, proves nothing by a homosexual encounter except that she has had a homosexual encounter—with any implication that may have in terms of a *human* encounter: tenderness, warmth, fear, whatever. But you cannot find your sexual identity through another person no matter *what* you are.

The pitch no doubt frightens many women away; also it preys upon the confused lonely woman. It has the aura of being one of the new Ten Commandments: the way, an article of faith. Actually it seems to me that women have been infantilized and tyrannized enough by close contact with their mothers; perhaps they have "known" women too long; perhaps the homosexual imperative is really an effort to get back to mother.

Here is what I mean. There is an apparent paradox about many of the self-styled feminists I have met socially and in my office. They are through with being fucked over by men; they want no part of men and they spurn all the customary visible trappings that make them appear like sexual objects—and the more they spurn makeup, skirts, and whatever else, of course the more they adopt male clothing. What I have found is that they don't want freedom from men at all. They want freedom from domineering mothers.

How to get away from mother? By not being *like* mother, by rejecting mother's traditional values and appearance. The apparent paradox is resolved when one understands that to avoid mother's domination as children, they turn to their fathers for love, acceptance, tenderness, and some sense of worth and identity. Except that father didn't come through. So that as grown-ups they are on some level neither women nor men, basically uncomfortable with both sexes. But why do men, rather than women, bear the full brunt of their conscious anger? Because you cannot break a powerful dependent bond with a mother without suffering anxiety and depression; nor can you break it via ideology, but only through understanding why the need still exists. A woman who uncritically obeys another woman's injunction to engage in *any* activity is essentially succumbing to mother's edicts; and if the obeyed injunctions result in something destructive, then she is being fucked over by a woman and not a man.

At the same time many women will say that mother, being a woman, was fucked over and so is not responsible for what she did to her daughters. And when you hear that particular kind of cop-out, you have finally discovered the real thrust of the anger, because to say that mother is blameless because she is a victimized woman is to dehumanize her, to deny any volition and freedom she may possess. That is a very special kind of anger: it is an existential, spiritual murder.

Speaking of anger, men usually have absolutely no idea of how wildly angry many women are. Because anger is out of the gestalt of "how to raise a girl so that she behaves and complies," women have had to find very strange ways, unconscious ways, of expressing it—which often cripples vital areas of their lives; such as:

Withholding sexual contact or having an affair without any real pleasure;

Being late, not listening to others when they speak, acting stupid when they are not stupid at all;

A general incompetence which subverts plans, plunges quite trivial activities into generalized chaos.

And many more—but usually around the theme of incompetence or silliness. Which lets the anger be expressed by thwarting others. But firmly in the context of how a "little girl" just *is*.

Reflection: There was Doris who didn't even know that she was angry, who could not recall one time in her young life when she had said so much as a cross word to man, woman, or beast. But when she became angry, although she did not know that she was angry, she would pull hairs from her head, sometimes one or two, sometimes in handfuls; maybe a barometer of a little anger or a big anger. When she ran out of hair and needed a wig her anger did not stop. But what she found were her arms. She could pick at the flesh, make little holes, tear small strips away. Eventually she found her legs, finally her face, and when nothing was left she could do only one thing. Vanish. Across both her wrists were the neatest, most precise cuts she had ever made.

Feminists frequently assert that the plight of woman is particularly reflected by the fact (and it *is* a fact) that more women than men are in psychotherapy. Not at all. It simply reflects that at this point in time women are probably smarter than men—or at least are more attuned to themselves. Almost every woman I have ever seen in psychotherapy—despite such problems as anxiety or depression—wants the same thing and can say so fairly quickly: to find out who she is, to discover the substance of her life, to feel alive, to connect in a human relationship, to explore a false role.

Many men ultimately want the same things—except for a long time they don't know it. They want initially to be more *successful* in their social roles—financial, career, sexual, the latter in terms of function and performance, not love. Which always confirms my feeling that men are more victimized by role. This is why so many men are frustrated, awed, perplexed by what a woman wants of them; they are very far from the core of themselves and have bought a social definition of their identities. Women have had nothing to buy even if they had the coin: nothing has been offered for sale. Yet this is an odd blessing. It allows women to seek freedom more directly.

Women who have accepted the roles laid upon them, who consider them real, are in utter despair and don't even know it; they cannot, in their profound fear, leave their roles, even look within themselves. *These* are the women who reflect the plight, not those who go to psychotherapy. Women in therapy reflect the dynamism of the woman of the future, the woman who understands that she must take life into her own hands.

Women in psychotherapy don't focus much on what they will achieve within their roles—meaning that they largely wish to be free of them. They have a greater desire for independence, but their relative lack of interest in acting their roles makes them already more independent than men. As I've said, men accept roles and feel neurotic if they don't fulfill them.

Of course, there are women who want to improve their acting skills: they are driving, success-oriented, terribly competitive. These are the women who appear "masculine" but really aren't; they simply associate themselves with traditional male values as a way of fleeing an onerous femininity.

Women in therapy have a variety of problems, but there is a major one which seems common to all women in or out of psychotherapy. Masochism. Not in the flamboyant sense of a scene set by de Sade, but in their posture of absorbing an almost unbelievable amount of sheer punishment at the hands of other people, men *and* women. Their ability to take it is, of course, a strength, but it is just about reflexive in the way they were raised: to be treated badly becomes equated with affection. To be treated well is almost frightening, and the man who treats them well is often perceived and condemned as weak. Because a sign of parental love was criticalness—attention paid in a negative way, the "good" girl who was good by passively absorbing, becoming a sponge. If you are this, and never assertive (nor angry), then you are loved. Even when a man does not want to be cruel, sadistic, dominating, such women try to force him into the position because they know no other real way to relate or feel love. A strange security—which often drives others away.

In essence, to many women love must be edged with some sort of disapproval. Again that element of being a child, and children in our society always stand perpetually in correction. And women will act like children—not with the "free spirit" of childhood—

but as dependent inferiors who on some level feel they deserve the punishment, the reprimand, the correction.

Do women become less masochistic during and after therapy? Certainly, but the price is tremendous anxiety—and then comes the point at which they must take responsibility for what they have done to others and to themselves. Masochism, being fucked over, is only one side of the coin. If you stop there, what you justify is that a woman is *exclusively* a victim—with the only task in life being to unvictimize herself and then all will be well. An incredible and damaging illusion. Because that is only the beginning; after that she must face herself.

Some women lately are falling victim to a particular kind of "psychotherapist" who is solidly in their corner—all feminist, women's lib dogmatist, who examines with a client not the full quality of her life, how *she* causes trouble, what *she* gets others to act out for her, how *she* defeats herself, but who emphasizes how she has been fucked over, deprived of her rights, manipulated. In short, *all* her difficulties result from being a woman.

This is reverse male chauvinism and it leads to reaction, not action, hollow rebellion and not autonomy of choice. The entire therapeutic line says that a woman is dominated by a man. It is also rotten therapy because it indoctrinates, leads, pushes—an authoritarianism in therapeutic disguise seeking converts to a cause.

This "therapy" plays upon anger and really lets the client do nothing for herself. It is a one-way communication that places a woman in a completely dependent position. With luck the woman may come to see such a therapeutic "technique" as just another form of demagoguery—and make a healthy break from the treatment.

To me, a moral is becoming clearer and clearer as time wears on. These days people just won't let women alone—especially other women.

Reflection: In our first meeting, Jennifer, twenty, tells me immediately that she doesn't know if she should have come at all because I am a man, and being a man I must be a Freudian with all that "penis-envy and women-are-supposed-to-be-passive shit." Her problem: all men ever wanted was her body and so why should she expect anything else from me? I arch my eyebrows at that.

"I mean, you might not want my body because you're a doctor and I guess you have some ethics, but you wouldn't mind if other men did and you wouldn't see it as their putting me down. You'd probably want me to get married, have a load of brats, and live for Chrissakes in Queens or someplace."

I tell her she can live in Tierra del Fuego if that's what she wants. She asks me what's in Tierra del Fuego, seriously, as if she's looking for a good place to move.

"Naked Indians who don't feel the cold."

"That's not for me."

"Me neither."

She laughs, says:

"You're off the wall."

"Me? Not me. I live in Queens or someplace, keep my wife barefoot and pregnant, and the first thing I thought when I saw you was 'Jesus, what a great person to have as a nice passive married-with-brats neighbor who could drop in and have coffee and envy my penis.' "

She laughs again.

"You really *are* off the wall."

I shrug my shoulders.

It turns out that Jennifer is tough, talented, resilient, appealing as a person, fun to be with, and a virgin—which she says is "weird." She is stuck the way so many girls in *my* generation were stuck: to avoid intimacy she does a *shtick* for every man she goes out with—an unabated flow of wit, repartee, philosophy, jibes at MCPs, challenges. Finally she admits that no men had *ever* wanted her body; they could never get out of the way of her words to even have the thought. She was aware of this all the time but had the need to phrase it so: "All men want is my body." She just had it slightly backward.

Being a therapist in the sexual revolution, I am often asked how I feel about therapists who go to bed with their female patients. The question makes one rather naive assumption: female patients will hop in the sack with their therapists at a moment's notice. Also, I never heard the *question* phrased in terms of a patient being male and the therapist female. Which betrays two ongoing social bigotries: patients are seen as dependent and without will (stigma one), but these patients are by definition women (stigma two).

I have, however, heard of female therapists seducing male patients—and homosexual seductions as well.

Anyway, I suspect that when I am asked the question, somebody wants to find out something about me. Here's an answer: the more we overemphasize genital sexuality, the more we forget that there are other ways to love.

Finally, at the risk of sounding anti-intellectual (which I may be becoming), I must say that I am not interested in debates—with women or men. I am tired of intellectual debates, because they lead nowhere and are usually excuses to compete and fight.

As I refuse to take the rap for keeping down blacks because I am white, so too will I not bear women's attacks because I am male. If a woman considers me a pig before she takes the trouble to know me, then I will not talk to her. If she wants *only* to tell me of her oppression and victimization, I will not listen. If she baits me, I will walk away. If she harangues me, I will also walk away.

But I will also walk away from a man, a black, a homosexual—anybody—who does these things. I won't fight or argue. To hell with it.

If a woman wishes to share her humanity with me, I will try to share mine with her—and we may like or not like each other. But only on that basis.

It benefits me not at all to keep a woman stupid and oppressed; it can only bore me. Sexual objects are dull. I have no interest in economically oppressing women. Nor do I want my wife to live a life of drudgery so that she can be bitterly dependent upon me.

But if women free themselves then I, too, am freer. Because there will be more real people to be with—and I, too, have the obligation to focus upon the ways that I am still imprisoned, and I have the obligation to change.

All this cant of victimization. We are getting talked out; *Ms.* magazine is running out of copy, and the admen are taking over: *You've come a long way, baby; now get lung cancer with the rest of us.* Shall we talk it to death, as my generation still obsesses over the Spanish civil war—or do we come at last, women and men, to meet as people?

This, to me, is perhaps the single most powerful challenge we must have the courage to face: do we have the guts to come together, explore, risk the collapse of our clichés, foolishness, and needs to blame? That is where the future *must* go—or we will have a reaction, turn around, and return to where it all was before.

8

Human Love
and the Pornography
of the Soul

We are still clinging to each other, the men and women of my generation, but much of our lives together is undefined now, ambiguous, even frightening. We have lost the traditional ways by which we once touched; the family unit has come unseamed, yesterday's values are today's sludge. We look at even our very young children and hope that they will go to college and lay off hard drugs and not get pregnant. The structure is shattered and we have helped to blow it apart—yet unaware that we have provided the fuse, if not the powder itself. We insist upon putting blame on external sources, but we cannot really find them—not really. And that contributes to the confusion and pain; we do not want to admit that we have gotten our children to break the rules that have unconsciously enraged us for so many decades. We will take credit when all goes "well," but we act as if we have played no role at all when we perceive that our children are *doing bad things to us*. We cannot understand what they are doing because we are not in touch with what *we* really want to do.

> Reflection: My friend, middle-aged, sits with his eyes adrift; his hair is graying and his face is tired from his prosperity. His seventeen-year-old daughter has just had a routine, successful abortion performed by the doctor who brought her into the world. My friend has already remarked on that irony, but what he is really struggling with is the inescapable fact that his daughter and her boyfriend have had sex. Associating randomly, he recalls diapering her, powdering her pristine vagina. That she has had intercourse terrifies him, shakes him, appalls him, while at the same time he tries to maintain his liberal position. And then, almost philosophical, he says, "You know what really gets me? The thought that everybody is screwing. Everybody. I got laid for the first time when I was twenty. In Canada. Honest to God. I went all the way to Montreal to find a hooker. Now everybody does it everywhere. I mean ordinary people."
>
> He stares out of the window, slowly shakes his head, mutters: "Jesus."

This example of the "new" sexuality is hooked firmly into the now ethos which, in the province of sex, is a double-edged sword, which my friend perceives as sweeping in huge blind circles like a scythe gone mad. (Not once did he consider the possibility that his daughter might be in love; only that she was "laid.") Perhaps, like all major and minor social revolutions, the "new" sexuality does seem a bit mad, and predictably it is beginning to stimulate reactions and counterrevolution. Not in what has been called Archie Bunker country: the Archie Bunkers have always been genetic reactionaries, with perfect logic equating sexual intercourse with pornography, fluoridation, black power, and anything else strange or threatening. But now they have lost the clout of a powerful church and a government that even they are reluctantly admitting has betrayed them—not because it has gone left, but because it has gone crooked and lost all credibility.

What is more important is that the middle-aged liberals who have loosed the "new sexuality" are beginning to reel with the knowledge that their children—like "everybody"—are "screwing." The vicarious quality is becoming real, too threatening, and *they* are joining the Archie Bunkers on shaky but common ground —and together they may well provide the thrust for a counter-revolution. Naturally, they will justify it in the language of their world views, censoring their own sexual wishes which are being acted out by their children.

Certainly one positive aspect of changing sexual attitudes is that men and women have some support if they wish to be freer. But what has also sprung loose, above ground, is a literal hurricane of public nudity, pornography of all sorts, live sex shows, fly-by-night "sex clinics," and what I have referred to before as the sexual trade papers. We are institutionalizing it commercially; it may be threatening us, but we continue to make a buck on it until we decide how to get rid of what we have unleashed. Meanwhile, we are also enthralled by it all; to most of my generation sex *is* pornography. We were raised not on sexual freedom but on dirty pictures, and we would not like to meet our daughter in the *Playboy* gatefold.

The new sexuality, as my friend tacitly implied, is brutally intimidating. The avoidance of sex was once a virtue; suddenly, it has become a hang-up. And the sword's double edge turns up this way: while *true* sexual freedom is desirable, the hip imperative to get laid and be un-hung-up has helped corrode the possibility of emotional connectedness. Now if a woman maintains that she must love a man in order to sleep with him, she is weird, she hasn't got it together, she is a female sexist. In many ways our new *alleged* sexual freedom is an additional barrier to emotional touch and human commitment.

Just about anything with genital apparatus can screw, but

aside from some parallels with animal behavior, if there is anything at all positively unique about human sexuality it is the potential elements of caring, commitment, and mutual emotional dependency. It is an exclusively human package, and at its best, its richest, it usually beggars adequate description. We have labeled all this *love*, and being human we talk a great deal about it.

Also uniquely human is our propensity to idealize love—and perhaps this constitutes our greatest departure from the purely animal, sexual, aspects of coupling. Obviously, this idealization has gotten us into a great deal of trouble, since we have treated marriage in a terribly unreal way which has brought disillusion, disappointment, and frustration. But the Church and the societies that have sprung from it have perpetuated this idealization, using it as a framework for sexual union mainly as a means of procreation. It has been a cruel con game, made even more vicious by diverse laws which only recently have relaxed: *marriage* has been important but never the *people* who marry.

The whole concept of idealization was probably given its most potent kick in the teeth by the sardonic rock music of the late fifties and early sixties. Yet while idealization was such a destructive force, preventing real relationships, the headlong rush into sexuality—which certainly appears to be totally unabstract—is also undermining real relationships. We have a remarkable ability to use any set of circumstances to avoid full commitment to each other.

The potentiality for a fulfilling life with the opposite sex has roots in what Freud called the Oedipus complex, but I am going to describe it in a very different way, as a relationship between parents and children in a fully human context, with sexuality only an aspect of the relationship—but an aspect that goes haywire when the basic connections are damaged or distorted.

In simplest terms, a boy learns to relate to women and understand the concept of women from the relationship to his mother; similarly, a girl learns what she thinks a man is from her father.

Later peer relationships only bring this deep emotional learning into behavior. What happens—and this undercuts the "sinister" implications of Oedipus, which anyway is not as sexy as one thinks—is that at first parents make some effort to help their children become human. Later children perceive that their parents are of different sexes, though they do not fully realize the full range of possibilities in this difference. This perception may be crippled in a unisex setting—a setting which, at least via lip service, has reached some level of serious consideration.

> Reflection: A young "liberated" mother and father are show-ing off their infant daughter to family and friends. The mother startles the older generation by a question, "I wonder what gender we should make her?" An old uncle counters, "You want gender? Look in her diaper, you'll find gender."

In a heterosexual setting, the mother becomes the boy's proto-type of woman, the father becomes the girl's prototype of man —for better or worse. In future relationships the parent and lover or spouse will have many features and personality traits in com-mon, even if these are not apparent on the surface. This is inevitable: one must learn of the opposite sex from somewhere, and the strength or weakness of future bonds, the overall quality of these bonds, will be contingent upon the quality of the parent-child relationship. For example, there is always something —positive, negative, or both—of the real mother in the wife or girl friend. Traits of a mother can also reside in a husband. And this, as we will see presently, holds true in homosexual rela-tionships as well: as with a heterosexual union, each partner is often possessed of a complex and mystifying amalgam of traits of both mother *and* father. Even when a person is consumed with the need to find a partner completely unlike a parent, the quest is largely futile.

So far my position should be clear: all fulfillments and dis-ruptions, emotional and sexual, between men and women stem from the nature of family life in the very early years. My generation, which has been owned too long, clutched too long, has attempted consciously to repeat this pattern with *its* children. We have been fixed on our mothers unconscionably past appropriate time and consequently have evolved a whole literature of antimotherhood. Failing to make an emotionally satisfying transition from mother to woman Out There, the only way we seem to be able to extricate ourselves from our crippling dependency is by complaining to our analysts or waging hollow attacks against parenthood. We want our mothers to let us go. We want their *permission* for freedom; we cannot simply take it.

The men of my generation are notorious, even legendary, for sexually turning off their wives after several years of marriage. While they blame the dull sameness of marital sex, the general boredom and apathy, the curlers in their wives' hair, bad breath —anything, really, to save face and rationalize—what really happens is that they begin, unaware, to experience in their wives those aspects of mother that I discussed before. Aside from a man's need for a noncompetitor, as soon as a woman is perceived by a man as an individual, a person with a life of her own—in short, an assertive human—he begins to feel like a little boy who is being controlled and dominated by a powerful mother. Sexual contact suffers immediately: to fully feel a sexual experience a person must be willing to give up control of his intellectual faculties. He must, for lack of a better word, regress. And if this regression is equated with feeling like a helpless controlled child—then sex goes.

The extreme intimacy of marriage on all levels triggers this avoidance response—from physical flight (away from home) to perpetual television-watching, to statements such as "I work too hard" and "I'm not turned on," to actual impotence. Frequently, the wife is called "castrating," but this is nonsense; the husband really perceives her as turning him into a child, he becomes a child, and he demonstrates it by losing or damaging his adult sexual potentiality. The perception of power in the woman is blatantly clear: a wife, in reality, cannot *turn* a man into a child even if she *is* a screaming bitch. He does this to himself. And usually he is aware of none of this.

I have never heard of a man who went limp with a woman who on some level reminded him of a warm, loving mother, a mother he does not conceive of as a controlling, dominant person. He can love her, make love to her, without the necessity to turn her into a sex object without an identity.

I think these basic elements cross socioeconomic boundaries, although unusual employment pressures and financial discrimination are morbidly corrosive factors in the family structure of minority groups. But the middle- and upper-middle-class families are different propositions: deprived of no rights, they destroy themselves. The driven husband is home too infrequently to provide a stable or *desirable* model for son or daughter; most middle-class children can't even *describe* their parents' jobs. The example is patently clear: home is where you sleep and drink but not really live; marital relatedness is a sometime thing. Left to its own devices, without the justification and rules of an external structure, there is no internal fix, no cement, that defines the marriage as a vital, continuous bond. And no amount of mandatory Sunday barbecuing or tossing a football at a small boy can alleviate a primary fact: home is where the flatness is, where the plumbing leaks in betrayal and the cesspool over-flows into the flower beds that someone else has planted. Monday is release: he goes to his fabled "exciting" job, she goes to the beauty parlor or Ikebana class at the high school adult-education program.

Reflection: They are each forty-two, and they thought they could be a great success, having been born under the same astrological sign. They are slowly consuming themselves in the dim flames of a marriage dying by attrition and have come to consult me. He has discovered her affair and retaliates by telling her of his. They live in upper Westchester County, own a $125,000 house, four acres, two cars, and a snowmobile, they hire a full-time maid, and their town is far enough away from New York City so that they can sometimes be separated at night if he works late. She tells him that their life together would not have atrophied had they searched for values instead of money. He stares blankly and tells her that their way of life is the way of life she wanted and that the weight of maintaining it has all but destroyed him, almost sapped his will to live. She says, "I never said I *wanted* to live this way."

"You didn't have to say it. But I remember one thing you did say."

"What?"

"That you would never marry a man who didn't have life insurance."

"*You* want to live this way."

"If I didn't work like a bastard you'd be back in the Bronx."

"I'd go back if that's what it takes."

"Yeah, sure."

"Don't patronize me, goddamn it. I mean what I say. We don't need all this."

"We're in too deep. Do you know what I owe?"

"*Owe*," she repeats.

For the first time in the interchange he looks at her. Intently. Says, "What does he do to you when you're in bed?"

She says, "Maybe we are."

"What?"

"In too deep."

They cannot describe their lovers in any way that might help you recognize them if you met: they are strangers who appear to demand nothing. To each other they are strangers who have demanded too much. They have spent their lives together acting *as if* they knew each other. They were never committed but they cherish the illusion that once they were. Bcause it frightens them to realize that they have been terrified of closeness. They also know nothing of their children except that their fifteen-year-old daughter is unpopular at school and their seventeen-year-old son spends most of his time locked in his room dreaming of Porsches. Eventually they opt to stay together and to continue their affairs. They stay together because there is no place else to go emotionally. They are "in too deep."

These people can offer nothing to their children; there is no sound prototype of family, commitment, love, or sexuality. Their children's awareness of what a relationship is comes from this marriage and they will believe that this is the way of it until they repeat it in their own adult lives or break loose and repair themselves. One is unpopular, the other dreams of power symbols in his isolation. They do not yet know that they have been *taught loneliness*, taught that while people come into proximity with each other they do not relate or touch emotional depths. Their parents are "in too deep," but in reality they have never been in it at all.

This is a burned-out family. Under any circumstances the battle to come to life would be incredibly difficult; it's almost impossible now since the parents have announced their mutual retreat. They seem to have been ironically correct about their astrological signs: the irony is that they are too much alike. One cannot stimulate the other to any sort of positive action. They are parallel lives never converging. These are people to whom *things* happen.

It is the partners in such burned-out marriages—isolates living under the same roof—that are patsies for the glittery hucksterism surrounding the "sexual revolution"—a con game that could not care less for the positive aspects of changing attitudes toward sex. It dangles the gold of sexuality without commitment, emotional involvements, or hassles. It is the old idea of the dirty picture, a real pornography of the spirit, and it reinforces isolated, lonely ways of life. Anything without commitment is a way of living life from afar. It is pure voyeurism—even when two people, or three, or four, appear to touch, there is a standing away from life. What this sort of "pornography" plays upon is not a person's need for sexual expression; it plays upon his basic alienation and deepens it.

In what is called hard-core pornography, the pure mechanization of the sex startles one. No one ever *likes* anyone else. (The end of the film *Deep Throat* implies an impending marriage between heroine and hero, but only because the hero will obtain a nine-inch penis via surgery.) Activity is generally frenzied as in most adolescent masturbation; names are unimportant; identities are unimportant. The fact is that the sex is utterly narcissistic. The faceless partner is a mirror, and what it reflects is the failure to transform self-preoccupation into love for a person Out There. A failure of familial love; a fear of involvement except with a fantasy. The true hard core of pornography is its requirement that nothing be real.

And there are parallels in actual sexual encounters: the fling in the massage parlor, the pickup in the bar, the short trick with a prostitute. Certainly this is sexual activity, but it is a far cry from sexual freedom. It is almost compulsive, and what it offers is an illusion that one no longer masturbates, that one is hip, with it. With *it*, but with no one.

I paraphrase an ad I read in one of the sexual trade papers. A woman seeking a partner writes: "French? Of course. Greek? If gentle." Maybe if her anus finds some gentleness she can develop it into a relationship.

Rather than sexual freedom, such ads reveal one thing: apparently Frenching and Greeking are not all that easy to come by. If truth be told, the sexual atmosphere is still crusted over by Victorianism and repression, and pornography caters to people's inability to satisfy their sexual needs directly—as it has since time immemorial. These are not the people who are reassessing their emotional lives and forging a new productive sexual ethic. These are the hucksters and their victims—generational contemporaries—who make fortunes, spend fortunes, on our continuing repression and inability to establish or maintain human contact—a unflagging devotion to the principle that if sex is sex then it must remain "dirty." And my generation thrives on this principle on both the selling and buying ends.

The repression occurred in the first place from efforts to split off sexuality from real human contact, and, if anything, this proliferation of commercialized sex—which also splits it off from real human contact—may well finally result not in the solidification of a new sexuality but in a new suppression. To prevent this suppression in the future we must believe in a self-evident fact: pornography is emotional junk and what happens to it is irrelevant. But very relevant is what happens to true sexual reform—from new laws to sounder ways of child-rearing. If the baby goes with the bath water, a kind of social tragedy will occur. Yet the baby often does go, so we may have to defend pornography wholesale, trusting that it will find its small corner as people come more alive. After all, the generation enamored of it is declining.

Vital here is that young people are not attracted to pimps and pornography. In fact, they seem to disdain them—even though this disdain may in part be an aspect of their intellectual uniform. On the other hand, while they stand self-righteously above it all—they may indeed *be* above it. Remember that they are hardly a celibate generation; they are, probably with burning envy, regarded by society as the sexually permissive generation par excellence. True, many have not made smooth transitions from family ties to love Out There, but their experimentation —usually in some context of encounter and confrontation—underlines their wishes to have it a better way. They populate therapy groups, especially encounter and Gestalt groups, and they often live together in random numbers—least of all for sexual reasons. They live together in arrangements different from what they perceive as the aridity of their parents' lives. In a profound way they are using therapy groups and their minicommunes as an emotional reeducation in a new kind of family. And sometimes it works. I have seen young couples in therapy struggle valiantly to live together with love and mutuality. Invariably they have sexual difficulties, but I am impressed by one fact: when basic problems of relating to each other as human beings are to some degree worked out, sexual problems decrease accordingly.

Reflection: These two are very different from the burned-out couple. They are not yet in their mid-twenties, have been married less than a year, and believe that their personal "hang-ups" are merging into a hung-up marriage. They are very definite about this: marriage has not caused their problems, nor did an astrological sign bring them together. They are driving each other away; they feel an actual sense of alienation, a sense of loneliness, whenever they are most intimate. Afraid of dependency, of losing themselves, they find their lovemaking suffers and they fantasize being with other people when they are in bed together. Sex, they say, is too often hollow, a sham, because they use instead of enjoy each other. They have discussed the possibilities of a "free" marriage, but they don't act on it because they trust something—what they feel as love, each for the other. They want to love each other all the way, and some three years later they will. I treat the husband and refer his wife to a colleague, and via individual therapy they get together by themselves. At home they explore together their inner lives, their fears, fantasies, hatreds, love, rage. It is a brave thing to do and they totter twice very badly, but they pull it together. Sex is the last problem I deal with, yet it is the thing that improves rapidly. Actually, the heart of it all is this: they have refused *not* to make it. And if this is the fabled stubbornness of youth, then the fable is worth elevating to legend.

These two are an example of what the sex therapists—the *legitimate* heirs of Masters and Johnson—know so well. That in order to attack a sexual problem head on, the basic relationship must be as sound as possible; or, as I heard one sex therapist say, the partners must not be emotionally "depleted." They must want to give to and gratify each other as people. But this is precisely why sexual therapy, though valuable, must remain somewhat superficial and limited in scope and applicability. The therapy is often simply a process of dealing with some residue of sexual shame and guilt, and many times only with a lack of practical knowledge. If two people cannot get close at all, if their basic mistrust of each other runs extremely deep, sexual therapy is not going to work. The disturbed sexuality is then only one symptom of a far more serious damage to the basic human being.

So I can state this: no person who is sexually free, sexually healthy, whatever term you choose, will marry or remain in a relationship with a person who is not. However, sexually disturbed people (as well as sexually free ones) will and do maintain relationships with each other; that is part of their usually tacit agreement, an agreement that frequently suffers and leads to a broken relationship when one partner attempts to clear up his disturbance while the other does not. By disturbed I really mean the relative inability to take pleasure and give pleasure to a *completely defined* other person; or a pervasive sense of sadness and isolation at what should be the peak of intimacy; or the need to turn the other person into someone else via fantasy, insisting on a certain kind of clothing, whatever; or just plain avoidance.

I am not talking about a woman's lack of orgasm; we don't know enough about that to make judgments. Many women experience sexual pleasure without that particular barometer—but if a woman cannot permit herself to get close to another person, then we *are* dealing with a disturbance.

Also, we have to acknowledge the fact that a great many marriages, despite so-called objective sexual problems, are successful. Sexual enjoyment and fulfillment are subjective, and within these marriages the partners have established their own norms. Nowhere is it written that sexual "health" is based upon a prescribed number of weekly or monthly sexual contacts. Yet I have often talked to people who become troubled by some piece of dubious "research" which states that the national norm for intercourse is two, three, or four times a week.

What I cannot repeat enough is that a disturbed marriage, which results in a disturbed family, is the product of each partner's individual problems—and most often each will not take responsibility for his own problems. The other person is "blamed," the abstract institution of marriage is blamed, and once this happens the floodgates open and any sort of action or behavior is justified. In our society sex with someone else is the usual result. The affair. The quick lay. The plaintive prelude of a trip to a motel: "My wife (husband) doesn't make me feel like a man (woman)." My generation uses sex this way really out of the need to feel alive, even loved—in short, to feel human. But it does not work. It is too steeped in illicitness and so remains "dirty." Another back door that opens on another dark corridor.

Conversely, there are many marriages and relationships that are structured almost completely on sexual lines, but most betray a profound undercurrent of isolation and fear. The emphasis on the physical in such relationships eventually results in morbid fears of aging, wrinkles, scar tissue from perpetual dieting, a horror of pregnancy, a lack of involvement with children—and if there are no children, a growing self-absorption, self-coddling, hypochondria. It is vital that these people remain youthful, attractive; they expect total rejection if they do not. Consequently, they fight the process of aging not only with cosmetics and dress that are bound to become age-inappropriate but also with fantasies of immortality. Sex gets to be increasingly fearful as age marches on and the inevitable expected rejection looms closer.

These partners are usually self-confessed isolationists—though they call themselves individualists. They will tell you that certain *personal* things are better left unsaid between husband and wife —whereas a true, committed relationship should be the ideal framework in which to express one's deepest thoughts and feelings. They are not at all interested in each other's personal lives and activities, though they are consumingly interested in the results of them: money, status, beauty. This, of course, is the quintessence of the narcissistic marriage; the focus is completely upon the superficial.

As for the family that emanates from this kind of marriage, the children become extensions of the parents. The mothers often dress their sons or daughters in exorbitant clothing that looks like a fully-iced cake; they wheel them around the neighborhood in crazily bedecked perambulators that resemble scaled-down Rolls Royces. The purpose is that everyone should gaze in awe at this *possession* of remarkable beauty. The fathers usually want male children to parade their virility; if the child is a girl they react with all the familiar narcissistic emotions: hurt, disappointment, resentment of both wife and child. The wife is regarded as if it is her fault that she could not produce a boy—and on an emotional level this is an exact parallel to the kings who banished or did in their queens for not giving birth to male progeny.

Actually, the wives in such marriages do not want children, wishing to retain center stage themselves. They will have them if that is what their husbands want, in order to keep the provisions flowing. These are usually the women who make every effort to deny childbirth. (Although the husbands want children, these wives are also deeply cognizant of such side effects as gaining weight, pain, all sorts of physical ugliness). They want to be doped senseless in the labor room; they do not want to participate in the birth. They never breast-feed, fantasizing some incalculable and irremedial damage to their breasts as sex objects; and at the same time they cannot tolerate giving anything of themselves—not even their milk to their own children. They would rather pump it into the bathroom sink.

The husband is king, the wife queen, and the children sometimes princelings. But beneath the surface they are all really children. Their children will remain children. They do not know who they are.

And no matter how beautifully the children are dressed, they will grow to be empty. Because the key here is *family* emptiness. Sex and love are never equated; indeed, there was never a real relationship to begin with. Being "loved" is looking good and maintaining a sexual desirability. In middle age, all the members of such families will try to restitute their youthful attractiveness by affairs with younger or "important" people. In *old* age, they simply die.

If marriage and the family are to assume a vitality in the future, relationships must develop in the direction of the young couple I mentioned before. Each couple must *redefine* marriage in the light of their own norms, redefining it according to the lives they wish to lead together as individuals. They may wish to separate —and if so, good. A marriage in which individuality is defined by a mutual agreement to have sex with other people is no marriage at all in the sense of an intimate relationship. Generally, if one partner extends this "permission" to the other, it is basically so that the other will not leave forever. Ultimately that corrodes. But the guise here is enlightenment, open-mindedness, freedom; actually it is a juggling act to avoid the responsibility of a relationship. Esthetically, too, it is stupid and hollow. Because in a profound sense, sexual contact with someone truly loved provides a dynamic emotional experience of intense beauty. This idea has deeply colored some of our greatest art, and if ever sex and love truly get together on the movie screen, the film will have incredible impact. No one will snigger like a "hip" New York audience at a showing of *Deep Throat*. People will be moved; they will feel something whether they admit it or not.

Probably at root every human being wants this sort of sex-love relationship, to *become* the other person. (Tristan: "I am Isolde."

Isolde: "I am Tristan.") But we have been largely crippled in our ability to establish it. We always *hope* to establish it. That is why the possibilities of marital sex and love have been so infused with romanticism—from the honest emotional yearnings of the past to the tawdry commercialization of a society that hires psychologists to tap deeper emotional needs in order to sell something.

But it is there, sunk inside of us, this need to fuse and merge our bodies with a loved person. No doubt it goes back into the unspoken depths of our contact with our mothers—perhaps even in the womb as well as out. But it is there, and we must come to recognize it, acknowledge it, *effect* it without fear. Anything less dehumanizes us, because turning away from a legitimate human need is to deny a part of the life within us. Yet a great question emerges. Are we brave enough to discover what we truly are?

Postscript: where life is held as cheap, every facet of human contact gradually cheapens until it becomes nothing. Our society has always paraded its attitude to human life as humane, progressive; in short, it ostensibly holds life dear, an ultimate value. But that is the facade—which cannot hide the corrosion so evident when we send our men into the military, especially when they occupy a foreign country.

After the fighting in Korea during the early fifties, life was drained of value. Occasionally you could find a body or two in the alleys; and gangs of children moved over you like a quick tidal wave leaving you sprawled in the street, stunned, your wallet and camera gone; and little boys would barter with you for their sisters or try to sell you tickets for "skivvy shows"—most often two women interminably locked in a sixty-nine position, flipping over now and then, signaling the flip with a slap on the back. There were "shows" in the company bars once a month, and the girls would be brought in via trucks from the

motor pool. A girl was a "moose." You took off Saturday
night to see your moose. What a moose wanted was something
from the Sears Roebuck catalog. In Seoul there were more
Sears Roebuck catalogs than Bibles and army training manuals
put together. A catalog for every moose.

I found a moose once as I walked up the dark hill to my
company. She was lying fetally, half in a ditch, a Sears Roebuck
dress torn off one shoulder, and she was crying. Maybe in a
year her face would be healed. The MPs came and took her
away, and while they lifted her gently into their jeep she kept
screaming as if something inside was broken. Probably she hadn't
been raped; you didn't have to rape anybody in Seoul. She was
just a moose who had annoyed her keeper.

Sykes was a mess corporal, and he had a moose, too, but
after a while you didn't see him with her very often, and then
not at all, and he got glum, withdrawn, and his hands began
to shake. And one morning a girl brought him a package wrapped
in a Korean newspaper, but he would not open it. It stank.
He began to babble, turning his body in short jerky circles,
then grabbed the package with one hand and a large kitchen
spoon with the other and began to dig a hole in back of the
mess hall. Furiously trying to dig a large hole with a small
spoon, whining through his nose. The stench of the package
seemed to worsen, but it was probably because by that time we
all knew what was in it. Finally he buried it, filling the hole
by shoveling in the earth with the sides of his shoes. Then stood
and stared, large uncomprehending eyes circling weirdly crimson.
Oh fuck, he mumbled, then began to beat his fists on the
corrugated iron wall of the mess. Wailing, *I want to go home.*
His first tender encounter with fatherhood.

And Howard, who soaked his suppurating penis in cans of
kerosene and gasoline because he was afraid that they would send
him to Headquarters Company and put him into a mythical
VD battalion. Meier's problem was that his VD was an exotic

"nonspecific" strain that the medic promised him might never be cured . . .

On party nights in the company bar, booze ten cents a shot, dancing was dry-humping, schedules worked out. Did your pickup moose have a good bed and did she live in an on-limits part of the city? No *kimchee* on the breath; no one wanted to screw surrounded by a cloud of garlic and fermented cabbage. My generation was becoming particular, gourmets of the moose. No guilt. The army let you do this. Camp followers were traditional; every army had them because the men needed them for morale.

And then. And then there was Riddle, who from all the rubble took the hand of a *girl*, not a moose, and in his inarticulate Georgia-cracker way, requested permission to marry her. Only God knows what bizarre rule Riddle broke—probably the cardinal rule he grew up with in the South. Only he wanted to marry a gook instead of a nigger. Reams of forms poured into the orderly room; I worked on them off and on for months. Whenever completed, they were returned to be redone. Finally I complained, and a voice I had never heard before said to me on the phone, "If you don't want to do those papers over, and over and over, well you just get his ass off the idea." Which I didn't, and he would come and stand in front of my desk with his fatigue cap crumpled in his hands and ask me how it was going, and one day when he knew how it was going, he disappeared. But of course they found him, and then there were court-martial papers, which get processed with the speed of light, and ultimately I don't know where he went because my time was over. They beat him, this man who had a girl, not a moose.

It was all a pornography of the soul. Because it is quite possible that he might have been in love.

9
Difference Is
a Matter of Choice

Consistent with the last chapter, I am going to write about certain aspects of homosexuality, mainly in the context of commitment and love. Because that is what homosexuals do: engage in contact as a means of finding their humanity. And it has little to do with sex. Unlike the stereotype that labels all homosexuals as closet queens, dikes, screaming faggots, or toilet cruisers—though certainly some are—homosexuals seek and avoid relationships and commitment with the same intensity as "straight" people. Or to flip the coin: just as homosexuality can sometimes be an escape from heterosexuality, the opposite is also true.

As I write this chapter, the American Psychiatric Association, despite some violent dissent, has decided at least temporarily to remove homosexuality from its list of mental-emotional disorders.[1] Perhaps this belated decision partly represents an honest shift in traditional attitudes and prejudices (shared with organized religion) toward homosexuality as a perversion (or a sin of perversion). But I somehow mistrust this overtly benign, enlightened move. Having been, and still being, close to the mental health establishment, I think the change emanates less from the inside than from intense public pressure. Certainly, we are seeing such phenomena as psychotherapists publicly acknowledging their homosexual activity and fantasies. And the facts remain that one cannot "treat" homosexuality and that most homosexuals do not *want* to be "treated." So I suspect that the establishment has opted to throw in the sponge before it begins to be laughed at. (How the American Psychoanalytic Association comes to view this we can only wait to see.)

Yet despite my feeling that this new position has a vague odor of duress and pandering, the crucial point is that the homosexual is no longer formally classified as "sick" by the arbiters of mental health and illness. Though I toss out still another caveat: blacks were "freed" a century ago. So while a significant step forward has been taken, homosexuals will have to hammer away at assuring their rights with unabated intensity. They will have to keep exposing and, if necessary, prosecuting the hypocrisy that oils the wheels of the larger machine which usually washes its hands like a mechanized Pilate.

There has always been a fascination about homosexuality—as there has been about any of our impulses and feelings that deviate from social approval. This sort of fascination always contains a hidden aura of attraction which we must struggle desperately to deny—though we rarely know *why* we must deny it except that we have been told to by overt and covert pressures.

Anything so unremittingly persecuted, even parodied by stand-up comedians, quite simply scares the hell out of most people. Many homosexuals have seen very clearly into this fear; namely, that possibly *the* major reason they have suffered such vicious attack and social ostracism, and are met with such repulsion and loathing by people who do not even know them, is that "straights" are really reacting against their own (often unconscious) homosexual impulses. What they fear, and thus must hate as a weakness within themselves, is objectified in the person of the homosexual. This is a kind of paranoia, yet we rarely label it as such.

Out of this swamp of fear emerges the foundation of an emotional power center on which rests the establishment's view of homosexuals as pariahs, plagues, neurotic—whatever. Yet, at the same time, society has always permitted some form of "homosexual" behavior so long as genital pleasure is not a factor: locker-room cavorting, brandy and cigars in the library, men's clubs, Holmes and Watson, the embrace permitted men in Latin countries. Women, on the other hand, have been allowed to express feelings for each other far more openly; they could always hug and kiss publicly, but it has been primarily since the women's liberation movement that some women see in this contact a veiled homosexual threat. In the past, such contact was divested of any "taint" of homosexuality because it was regarded as dependent and childlike—making it a contact not between adults but between children. Again, woman as perpetual child. Until quite recently, descriptions of sexual contact between women stressed a cuddly, clinging quality: bodies were stroked, orgasm achieved without much direct manual or oral stimulation.

Men still avoid this childlike quality with all the panic of a hare fleeing the hunter, because they tend to equate any feeling of dependency with weakness, vulnerability, a violation of the masculine role, and ultimately, on an unconscious plane, with homosexuality. This seems especially true in this country: the stereotype is the World War I or Foreign Legion film where a French officer decorates, then kisses the cheeks of, Gary Cooper or a reasonable facsimile. With confused, popping eyes, the hero always acts vaguely raped. Or goosed. This is a required reaction to the "homosexuality" of foreign customs; it preserves the American way of virility. Of course, this Gary Cooper shock is *never* taken as the hero'^ problem; it is the Frenchman who is slightly gay. Aren't they all?

Largely as a by-product of this generation's thrust toward feeling, more men are embracing and kissing cheeks in public (lip contact is forbidden either sex) and there are all sorts of reasons for it: true affection, exhibitionism, testing some new way to show feeling, maybe having discovered something in group psychotherapy or at the local guru. But they are doing it. Conversely, women, who have always hugged and kissed, are beginning to talk to each other, getting their heads and ideas out of the kitchens and nurseries, finding that their intellectual competence extends past shaving a carrot with the proper utensil. Crippling roles are beginning to crumble: a person may yet become a person first. A *person* who happened to be born male or female. Of course, we have to beware of our traditional American tranquilizer: commercialization. Male clothing is brighter, hence more expensive; purses for men will momentarily arrive on the shelves of Gucci—turning yesterday's faggotry into tomorrow's profit. And every television viewer must realize how *intelligently* and *informatively* women are discussing toilet-tank cleaners and buying products in those "candid" ads because the new product is more effective than the old. Now women are smart. Katy Winters, where are you?

De-symbolizing all this, why should anyone care how anyone else conducts his or her sex life—or with whom? Aside from some validity in the biological point of view that sexual intercourse originated as a means of propagating the species (instinctually animals *must*, but we are not so bound), absolutely no rational, intelligent case can be made against homosexual love, and certainly none in favor of its suppression in any form. Not if there is one shred of belief left in the human being's capacity for free will, which in less abstract form I call the capacity to choose based upon the ability to perceive alternatives and possibilities. Specifically, while a person may be propelled into homosexuality by personality factors removed from awareness, he or she may also choose it with awareness. The same holds true of heterosexuality: there are people who *must* be heterosexual, like Don Juan who was not able to commit himself and whose goal was conquest rather than sexual pleasure or love. The psychiatric establishment has in the past utterly disregarded factors of choice—choice being a province of the "ego" and hence a sign of health. Homosexuality has been viewed as somewhat of a compulsion, a "defense," and therefore a symptom or syndrome.

Perhaps this sounds as if I am saying that a person must try all sorts of sexual experiences in order to come to some honest conclusion about the way he wishes to go. Obviously this is true for some people—but that is not the major point. Again I maintain that the *kind* of sexual contact is secondary to the human *quality* of any relationship—that is, what one seeks in it or derives from it in terms of growth, truth, openness, responsibility, affection, and a sense of being alive. At times, sexual contact is almost irrelevant; the contact may be purely a search for a different sort of human touch.

Reflection: He is a brilliant young chemist, creative, narcissistic, and he cannot communicate with laboratory supervisors; he was once dropped from a college faculty following a clash with the department head. He consults a therapist after a broken love-hate relationship with a dynamic successful businesswoman whose sexual "demands" he countered with impotence. On the night the relationship ended he "found" himself walking in a park, then "found" himself being picked up by a homosexual. He repeated the experience a number of times, yet does not "feel" like a homosexual. Somehow it doesn't sit right; his sense of it all is that he is looking for something else.

One afternoon he asks his therapist to go for a walk in a nearby park "just to get out of the office."

The therapist immediately agrees. He knows that the young man had never been close to his father although he had always wanted to be close. He also knows that his patient had been all but overwhelmed by a dominating, controlling mother who scorned his masculinity and who had actually made fun of his "little thing." (Publicly she was quite submissive to her husband, the pastor of a Lutheran church.) The therapist recognizes a deep repetitive pattern: after being rejected by his fiancée, the young man tried to turn to men for affection as he had unsuccessfully attempted to turn to his father. In the park he felt wanted by a man; sexual pleasure had nothing to do with it.

Another therapist might have refused the walk and dealt with the homosexual implications of the request. This therapist penetrated the layer of ostensible homosexuality without any verbalization whatever. So they walked in the park, had a beer, watched a few innings of a softball game, and not once did any *obvious* therapeutic interchange take place. Except that every moment was vibrantly therapeutic. They discussed sports, commented on a pretty girl or two. In short, the therapist was not a character in a *sub rosa* homosexual fantasy. He was a man—admittedly in the part role of an accepting father, but also a man in his own right.

Within several months the young man no longer felt a need for homosexual encounters. Finally he could choose.

Another man could have chosen to develop his homosexual encounters into a way of life, a way of human commitment. But the young chemist did not. To do so would have been false, because for him homosexuality did not, never would, "feel right."

On a broader societal level, what is exceedingly valuable about the gay lib movement is not only the provision of a forum of support for homosexuals who wish openly to pursue their rights as members of the human race. More than that, it will help to get sexual contact out of subway toilets—which is not where human touch belongs. (There will always be quick clandestine sex between homosexuals as well as "straights," between anyone fearful of real emotional involvement.) In opening the closet doors the movement will invite a crucial test: whether or not homosexual couples can make it together. This is no idle piece of social research; it is probably the single most important area to explore, and the results will have stunning implications for the future of all authentic human relationships—because most homosexuals have never been free to initiate and maintain a relationship in any sensible, decent way, either in process or permanence, thus discovering if it prospers or founders upon the structure of its own quality or lack of it. (Nor have heterosexual couples so long as marriage has been a social imperative. In both cases the element of choice has been undermined by social values and mores.) For the homosexual pair life has usually been lived in secrecy or subterfuge—or, if open, subjected to the most vicious pressures of a hostile environment. Only exceptionally strong and courageous human beings can withstand this pressure, but people should not be forced to exhibit such courage in the disposition of their personal lives. It is a courage we could well do without.

Stereotypically, the homosexual relationship has been widely viewed as doomed to failure, while the irony is that in almost no case has society given it a fair chance to succeed. The majority of straight marriages in this society are overwhelmingly threatened by corrosion and instability; why then must homosexuals suffer this accusation? But there has always been a quick out: homosexual relationships *must* founder *because* they are homosexual. This is idiocy, and pernicious as well because it is a facile and silly point of view promulgated by establishment "straights" in lieu of any reasonable rationale. The fact is worth repeating immediately that homosexuals are not even provided with a soil in which to sow a relationship. The prediction of doom follows from prejudgment, and orthodox psychiatry and religion have been bastions of this prejuice, that is, that there is a specific reason that homosexual unions founder when they founder. The reason, says the myth, is homosexuality—and consistently I know very few psychotherapists who will do couple-therapy with homosexual partners, although they will "treat" homosexuals but mainly those who wish to become "straight." Old line therapists are generally loath to or outrightly refuse to treat homosexuals who wish to remain homosexuals. But when a marriage goes on the rocks, heterosexuality is never fingered as the culprit. Never, because heterosexuality has never been officially listed as a diagnostic category; problems within the relationship are dutifully discussed and therapy marches on. Quite simply, homosexuals have never been regarded really as people.

As I mentioned before, it is common knowledge that in a heterosexual relationship a man may look for attributes of his father in his wife as his wife may seek qualities of her mother in her husband. Psychotherapists have always accepted this but have rarely, if ever, criticized the concept of heterosexuality per se. Conversely, when they discover such unconscious searches in same-gender couples, they point to the impossibility of homosexual unions. They seem blind to the idea that *sexuality* may be a completely *secondary concern.*

Reflection: They are two youngish homosexual men, vastly talented and successful, and their relationship is rocky. Their sexual life is suffering, but there is something more profoundly unsatisfying in the way they communicate and live together. It is difficult to give to each other. They know that interpersonal competition is corrosive, but they compete although there is nothing in reality to compete with. Both are in different fields, both are admired and respected in these fields, both their professional milieus have a high degree of tolerance for homosexuality. They don't know why they compete. They don't even consider the idea that homosexuality is *the* problem, and they are right. It is their conviction about this that provides the impetus to probe the more hidden aspects of their relationship. They begin to talk, open, interact, and a bald fact becomes startlingly clear. They have the same "transferences" as a straight, married couple; even good friends who do not have sex together could have these unconscious distortions in their perceptions of each other. Their sexual problems are only reflections of something more basically disordered. Hidden in their relationship are expectations that cannot be fulfilled because they are rooted in fantasies, in distortions. Each sees the other as a powerful, humiliating, dominating, manipulating parent, and they come to see that those perceptions have little to do with reality but that they create fears of intimacy and hence of sexual contact. Paul is tired after a day's work, hates to talk shop. Tony unconsciously equates this with his stony father's coldness, withholding, and secrecy; he tries to get through this "wall" he perceives in Paul as he tried with his father—by asking questions. Paul sees this as his mother's nagging, her incessant impingement on his privacy. Their relationship contains many such unconscious warped interactions, and despite their intelligence they cannot focus on what is really going on because when they are locked into this together, they cannot see what is going on. Just like any two people locked into a distortion. When they begin to gain awareness, things improve; they begin to sort out, identify, their childish reactions and expectations. After some tentative approaches intimacy improves; the word *compete* vanishes.

Where we are headed here is very consistent with the growing awareness that, in general, human factors are far more important than purely sexual factors. Sexuality—though obviously gender differences are important—has been for too long the proving ground of male and female identity; there are other ways of assessing identities, including differences and similarities between the sexes. And there are more important ways of assessing the quality of relationships—one way, of course, is by asking the people involved, but we rarely do that where homosexuality is concerned. For example, since marriage, a male-female bond, has occurred with such frequency *thus far in history*, we have insisted that it is a norm. Based on the science of statistics, it probably is. But what of it? One might say that since people buy automobiles built with planned obsolescence, it is then a norm to buy obsolescent cars. Which it is, because so many of us do so. Yet that doesn't mean that it is rational or "good" or that the norm will remain a norm. Norms are tricky but there is one fact inherent in them: they are intrinsically value-free, unless one infuses them with a personal value system which makes them good or bad. In fact, they just show that a lot of people are doing something. Like wearing a tie to work.

Society places one value judgment ("good") on the norm of heterosexuality and another ("bad") on homosexuality. No judgments are placed on the countless other norms that do not threaten us with potential exposure of our repressed inner lives. Nevertheless, norms are the backbone of our socioeconomic-educational lives; norms sell products, give us security, pressure us into conformity, crush dissidents, dictate curricula. But one rarely chooses to be a statistic in the norm; one sort of falls into it. A movement of least resistance.

Sometimes there is a search for norms, and that is what science is partly about. It wants to predict firm norms and, when it can, that is what science is *all* about. For Freud the Oedipus complex was a universal norm; a "successful" resolution of it would lead to the universal norm of heterosexuality. But based upon the incredible deviations from the Oedipal situation, it can only be a norm in the abstract—a fantasied norm, a wish. The resolution is supposed to *happen* to a child; he or she falls into the norm of heterosexuality. But I think it is more complicated than that. The only means by which we know that the resolution has been "successful" is if we use the barometer of heterosexuality —and that is circular. It may even be a fiction. But it is what most of us wish to believe, and we have believed in illusions for centuries.

Consistently, psychology and psychiatry have for decades attempted to find what "went wrong" in the development of children who later became overt homosexuals. And this "research" has been done primarily with males—a fact that reflects what lies close to the heart of a so-called sexist society. That is, whatever threatens maleness (including female homosexuality) in its stereotyped version is stamped as deviant, emotionally aberrant, and consequently fit for research aimed at prevention and cure. Scientists and hard-hats simply use different approaches: the goal is remarkably similar. There has even been a theory of "pseudohomosexuality," [2] which on one level attempts completely to defuse the sexual aspects of homosexuality and to get the person into bed with the opposite sex. *Human touch* is not even a consideration. Often the concept is used to convince a male patient that he uses homosexual fantasies to escape women, which is certainly possible; but any gratuitous introduction of this idea into therapy might tell you more about the therapist than the patient.

The result of all this "research" has been next to nothing. It has probed and catalogued parental personalities: cold, removed fathers plus overprotective mothers; physically brutal fathers plus weak, fearful mothers—combinations ad infinitum. Yet we have learned very little about homosexuality. You can find the same combinations working their effects on heterosexuals, which to me simply underlines the old obvious fact that there is a mixture of sexual characteristics in all of us, and that inadequate parenting damages our capacity for intimacy regardless of what our overt sexual orientation may be.

Psychiatry, however, has usually bent on one point—that in certain military or prison situations men may engage in homosexual activity without the stigma of sickness or deviation. They do so only because no women are available, hence forming a mininorm which makes it "all right." Whether these men want sexual release or human warmth and intimacy, we don't really know. Perhaps both. But notice that the *absence of women* is the key phrase—not the availability or desirability of male contact. This keeps homosexuality a pathological entity when women are available; yet by a probably unintentional irony it emphasizes that the potentiality for homosexual behavior exists in every man (and woman). And it shows that people seem to need permission and justification—social sanction—in order to let such behavior emerge. Thus, when the closet doors are fully opened there will be a greater number of homosexual unions—and this will certainly create deep fissures in a sexist society. Because men have used women as vehicles to deny their homosexuality and prove their masculinity. I am not sure that it works so powerfully the other way around.

Reflection: The army again. Korea, where homosexuality was a dangerous game, where a stay in a mental ward might earn you a chart at the foot of your bed that read: HOMOSEXUAL. Where you could be court-martialed if caught. Where you were obviously sick because so many mooses were available to play with. He was a black man, a sergeant, tall, with remarkably expressive eyes and sensitive mouth, and the combination of his good looks and sergeant stripes attracted crowds of women at company parties. He was affable and, for the time and the place, almost weirdly courteous, and would let a girl choose him, then sit with her and treat her like a very special date. Attentive, interested, a bit aloof; unlike most, he knew enough Korean to keep a rudimentary conversation going. But he never went home with a girl, simply helped her into the truck at evening's end and said good-bye. I understood him, though, only when accidentally I saw him in Tokyo on leave. In a dark bar off the Ginza, just two booths away, he sat with a Japanese man. Attentive, interested, but more alive than with a girl. And then I saw something that I had never seen before in my life: slowly they embraced and kissed. On the mouth, romantically, lovingly. I left, turning my back so that he wouldn't see me, afraid that he would be afraid. Months later we would have another kind of "meeting." . . .

I don't think that the social mess surrounding homosexuality will be fully worked out by members of this generation—though they are shaking the hell out of things largely via their pursuit of intimacy and contact while letting the sexual chips fall where they may. Perhaps they are not as laissez-faire sexually as they say they are, but so long as people think they are, something happens, juices get stirred. They have probably performed their greatest service for homosexuals who are in their thirties and forties, since these seem to be the people who are shunting off their shroud of secrecy. My generation, of course, has also invested rather heavily in the homosexual pornography market, thus giving permission in this area as well as in the "straight" area. Book publishers and film makers are middle-aged entrepreneurs who exploit the efforts of real people seeking freedom of expression, while they themselves are getting others to act out their own homosexual wishes—or at least wishes to get away from women. The debasement is almost primitive: freedom to love as one wants is converted into freedom to "fuck around."

My generation has also perpetuated the stereotype of the closet queen and the toilet queer and the screaming fag. The creepier and more sordid the better; every effort is undertaken to visibly separate the "men" from the fags. And this, too, has become a norm in its own way, and a number of homosexuals have flaunted it by adopting it. They can be flamboyant, swishy—driven to this kind of lunacy by the need to rebel, to extend a rigid middle finger at the "straights," to upset them, even to stimulate them. Some just simply don't give a damn any longer.

"Straights," especially male "straights," flaunt as well; but we rarely, if ever, call it that. *Machismo.* Tarzan. They need the world to *see* their heterosexuality just as they need the world to see homosexuals. The two mustn't ever be confused. I have mentioned that their unremitting sexual activity serves often to ward off homosexual thoughts or feelings; they will parade beautiful women through the streets, exhibit them at cocktail parties, without the vaguest awareness that they may also be using the women to attract male attention. Take away their women and they begin to feel anxious, uptight, ill at ease; they have no other way to prove their manhood.

Now homosexuals, as I have said, frequently see through these masks and are condemnatory and accusative—an "I know you" posture. This is understandable; blacks, another minority group, focus anger on whites in general. But unless man's incredible ignorance of himself is handled with more gentleness, there will be a powerful reaction which is really avoidable. Homosexuals may be aware of their homosexuality, but they can be as stupid about themselves, blind to their own inner forces, as anyone else —thereby not knowing if what they are doing *is* choice or compulsion. In line with this is the rather smug "challenge" that if two men or two women are intimate friends, their relationship *must* be consummated sexually. Or that if a person has conscious homosexual fantasies he must act upon them or else admit his inauthenticity. This is a thinly disguised case for homosexuality as the only true form of sexual contact—and the whole matter of personal choice is omitted in a batch of imperatives as rigid and off the point as the claim that heterosexuality is the only way of the world. Actually, awareness is the great liberator: if men and women know that, like all their compatriots in life, they have the capacity for all sorts of sexual feelings, *then and only then* are they free to choose the means of expressing these feelings. And if we do not choose, then we conduct our lives with the dumb, instinctual rigidity of an earthworm or fly. Besides, I am convinced that homosexuals who espouse and proselytize their way as the only way have a desperate need for rationalization and justification. They are wearing their homosexuality uncomfortably. It is more important, vital even, to keep homosexuality close to the forefront of social reform rather than to carp at the fakery of "straights." Out of the closets, homosexuals must stay out—or plunge back into paranoia.

Reflection: This young homosexual man is very frightened and he describes himself as becoming—and he uses the word—paranoid. He believes that sometimes he is being watched and followed; he doesn't know by whom. What is really happening is that he is being blackmailed by a co-worker. Not for money, but with the threat that if he does not decline a competitive promotion crucial to his career his co-worker will expose his homosexuality and he will be fired. The young man feels that all his activities are being observed in order to gather more evidence against him. After some discussion and exploration it emerges that he has been scaring himself: the co-worker has probably never seen him in any sort of homosexual situation, simply implying, guessing, latching on to some effeminate gesture, some slip of the tongue—which people who must hide anything so important frequently make. But the young man cannot take the risk of telling him to go to hell. He explores further and knows concretely that he could never have been observed in homosexual activity; he has hidden it too well. Moreover, his doorman has made some sly *macho* comments when he brings home a young woman for after-hours work on a project they share. Eventually he is relieved. But then he breaks down and cries —no longer because of the exact situation but because of the incredible strain of secrecy, a strain that has caused him to have minimal social contacts for fear of discovery. A man driven deep into secrecy, driven away from relationships with all sorts of people.

I think that I have pointed clearly enough to the direction homosexuality may well take in the future, barring some vicious social reaction. But I want to close this chapter with a speculation for the far distant future, and it has much to do with the human race's innate potentiality for self-control, self-policing. As lesser animals and insects achieve—when allowed by man—a natural balance built around both a drive for survival and a propensity for self-limiting population growth, so too must man. I do not believe that we will achieve our balance via the technology of contraception or by our use of technology to destroy ourselves in an orgy of ecological suicide. Having invented our technology, we can always manipulate it should the real threat of extinction loom large. That we cannot do this is the content of the poetry of doom. Perhaps at one time we limited ourselves, balanced ourselves, by wars that were *actually* fought in the context of real territorial imperatives; but now we fight them for such abstractions as turning back the tides of ideological encroachment. Is that just as real as Caesar's legions incorporating real estate into the empire of Rome simply because we can think and hence make abstractions concrete? Not at all: thought does not equal deed no matter how desperately we might insist that it does. No, we are still too much the animal; we cannot pretend that we have utterly severed ourselves from the beings that emerged from the primal ooze. We are simply animals who *can* think. When we learn really *how* to think, then we will become a bona fide species. As Homo sapiens we are just as unstable, in flux, as once was the ant before he became Ant, the lion before he became Lion.

So I will follow an obvious fact with a speculation: while I believe that homosexual love can be a genuine human love of great emotional depth, it does not produce progeny. Homosexuals simply do not bear children. I believe that certain kinds of homosexuality are probably constitutional. Even genetically determined, if you wish. And the purpose of this determination is to limit our tendency to overpopulation so that the species may survive. Deep in the genetic code, it exists: no mechanism to deprive us of our need for love and physical contact, but a mechanism to prevent overpopulation with unerring efficacy as there exists the mechanism of sperm plus egg equals offspring. Before this emerges full flower, this natural means of balance, perhaps we have effected it to some extent through infertility, stillbirths, miscarriages, abstinence, anything that naturally aborts or prevents. But there will come a time, which *we* will not see, when population will be limited by the inability to populate. And if one day we require more people? Then heterosexuality will again gain ascendance.

Why else are we the only species born into such a long dependency upon our parents? A dependency that causes the child to identify with the sexual characteristics of both mother and father. In essence, why else are we born in a soil guaranteed to nurture the seeds of bisexuality?

Postscript: Discreet though he was, the black sergeant with the expressive eyes was found one day caressing his Korean lover. He was taken by four enlisted men to the shower room at two in the morning, stripped, tied, and gagged. For an hour they intermittently urinated on his face. Then menaced his penis with a razor blade. But they didn't cut. And what he did when they finally released him I learned the next morning.

"He cried," I was told. "The motherfuckin' nigger just cried."

10

The Human Commitment
of Psychotherapy

Everything that has gone before in this book has emphasized that life is with people. So, too, the patient-therapist relationship; it is a vibrant human interaction. Changed perceptions of this relationship have been revolutionary and they are here to stay. The hunger for emotional contact, the quest for self-awareness, have radicalized both practice and theory and shaken traditional beliefs to the core. The impact has been obvious in the burgeoning of the humanist position and in the proliferation of the newer therapeutic modalities. But it is probably felt most sharply by therapists who are still convinced that the main thrust of communication is achieved via "talk" and technical wizardry—even though a great deal of significant research indicates that patients attribute their progress to the *human* qualities of their therapists.[1] In essence, the one-to-one relationship that exists in the consultation room is being vastly altered—and with it the image of the "patient" has been refocused in similarly dramatic terms.

The person who seeks therapy is being less often regarded as sick, neurotic, abnormal—except among the diehards of the psychiatric and psychoanalytic establishment. This shift has been one of the main contributions of humanistic psychology, even behaviorism, and certainly of the early works of Ronald Laing. As a result, psychiatry is fast losing its status as arbiter of mental "health" and "illness." The majority of people are no longer viewing their very human struggles in these contexts. And they are correct: there is something intrinsically dehumanizing about attaching a diagnosis, a traditional label of sickness, to one's fears of mice—or even one's fear of people. The "patient" is beginning to be seen as a person who wishes to *grow* and to be free, not to be "cured." Once this view is accepted, the therapist becomes a facilitator of a movement process rather than a doctor who attempts to heal. He becomes aware of his patients' humanness, not their "sickness." (There are, of course, those people in acute distress who are called psychotic. They are usually medicated, locked up, controlled; but the truth is that none of those measures really works very well.)

Another change occurs in the therapist: he now begins to realize that psychotherapy is a process of intense reciprocation. Therapist and patient share many things in common (even "psychopathology"). They feel with, and learn from, each other —a learning that transcends training and technical skill. An emotional learning.

Often in this book I have put quotation marks around the word *patient*. The term has lingered on from medical models of illness, implying that not only is the person in the less spectacular armchair ill, but that he or she is one down, dependent, weaker, unresourceful, unattuned to something called *reality*. The term no longer applies. But as long as we believe in its applicability, an abyss is created between the person and his therapist, a separation that is not only unreasonable, but one that simply does not exist. And as long as we therapists willingly use it as a definition, we are stigmatizing the person who consults us, while elevating ourselves. Yet as I suggested before, many of us need that illusory edge; some of us need it to function; some of us have dropped out of the field when we realized that we did not have it; and some of us have maintained that the edge is a given since the therapeutic relationship is "different" from other relationships, somehow artificial.

It *is* different, unique even, but it is not artificial—the main difference being that the therapist generally does not reveal the facts of his life as fully as the patient does. These days therapists are certainly more open, more interchanges take place, than ever in the past. There is a growing freedom in the way a therapist conducts himself; actually, even without verbalizing a therapist reveals a great deal about himself if anyone cares to see. For instance, some of my patients know that I have written novels and some do not; several have read them, several have not—deliberately. By avoiding my books they are avoiding me, and I must assume that they have difficulty knowing anyone. Because my fiction is deeply self-revealing: it is a powerful reflection of my inner life, my fantasies, my values and ethics, the way I see the world, feel it, and react to it. The same holds for this book; and some will read it, some will not.

There are other ways by which my patients know me: I have a fondness for anecdotes, metaphor, little stories—all of which reveal some aspect of myself. I don't use these anecdotes deliberately to entertain; I use them to elaborate or clarify something about the person who sits in the room with me. I speak to the person through the medium of my fantasies and ideas; but always *to* the person.

My patients also know me through my moods; by the pictures of my children framed on my desk; by the style of my furnishings and clothing; by the way I interchange with people in the waiting room; by how I sit. They can also gain a particular kind of insight into my personality by the fact that I have had in my office, for at least three years, a broken swivel chair.

I have never had a patient who asked me directly about the details of my sex life, the quality of my marriage, or how I raise my children. But if it helps to tell them something of my personal life, then I will do so—but only if it helps. Because what is important is not that we sit together, exchange factual details, and pretend that this is communication. Of real importance is that we get in touch on an emotional, human level, because that is where the truth is, where the distortions are, the bedrock of life, the heart of a relationship. On this level equality exists and the person as "patient" (I use the word for lack of better) is no longer a viable, relevant, or tenable concept. People are people, but three-dimensional only in an emotional context. I stress this idea unremittingly because so often we think that we are communicating with another person when what we are really doing is sorting through a catalog of facts, details, occurrences, and generally inoffensive opinions. But we aren't touching, we aren't knowing. In this sense the therapeutic relationship can be the most authentic relationship in our lives—at least for a time. I mean authentic for both patient *and* therapist. We get to know each other quite deeply by striking chords of the music that binds us as human beings; and this does not preclude dissonance and atonality.

One question that patients often *do* ask—in a variety of ways —is if the therapist likes them. (I suppose there are therapists that don't like their patients, in which case the patients are unconsciously urged to act out self-destructively; at best, such therapists hate themselves and their work, and their patients leave.) This is an important question since it tells you that many people acknowledge that they engage in human contact where little affection exists. One needn't answer it directly, because a person must explore its ramifications and arrive at independent conclusions. The question exposes so much of what is artificial, shaky, and mistrustful about human relatedness in general. A patient will worry that you might subtly lead him down the path to doom—and rightly so. At the same time he wants you to help him grow—also subtly, reflexively, whatever. The point being that he is *fearful of doing what you want him to do without his knowing it*—precisely the point I have been making all the while about unconscious communications of a relatively destructive kind. Everyone fears them, knows they exist. But no one cares if he knows or fully understands the process by which he begins to live more fully.

The question also indicates that most of us don't know what others really feel about us. We say certain things, do certain things, and we receive feedback of one sort or another; but we don't accurately know what lies deep in the heart of the other person. Our lack of faith in superficial positive feedback reflects our disenchantment with the social norm of polite exchanges. (Actually we know that if we ask another person if he likes us, the odds are overwhelming that he will say yes whether or not he really does; anyway, he doesn't believe that we mean the question seriously in the first place or it would make him too anxious.) This is why so many people who pass through our lives appear to "break character," vanish, end contact, even turn on us. Because we haven't really known them, nor they us; we have been playing a hollow social game. For this reason so many "patients" find it difficult to relate to "nonpatients." They complain of a lack of openness, a guardedness, a kind of patter larded with stock phrases and predictable attitudes. People not in therapy are probably not even remotely aware of this; but others who have come to appreciate spontaneity and who experience joy in relating freely feel bored when they must talk of books, plays, politics, inflation. They recognize that although the content of the books may be different, that the political cast of characters may have changed, they have had the same conversation every week of their lives.

Reflection: One of my patients describes this feeling beautifully.

He says, "It's all like a Victorian dinner party. Everything goes off like clockwork. The food is good and served well, the people smile, everyone talks, and they all tell you what a good time they've had. But there's something about it that you just don't believe because there isn't a damn thing else that anyone can say."

It is this kind of recognition, usually subliminal, that has brought to the coffee tables of the most reputable gatherings the inevitable cache of marijuana.

Being *with* someone, feeling alive with someone, becomes the goal of people seeking self-awareness. The goal is communicative gratification, and to achieve it people must touch on deeper levels, not merely talk. When such contact occurs there is something childlike about it. Childlike in the sense that honesty and openness pop through the facade, the posture that we mistakenly regard as adult behavior. It is emotional and basic; perhaps it is love, equality, security, a sense of acceptance.

These things are what any "patient" must feel from his therapist in order to take a chance in a relationship with another person; he must feel them from his therapist because he never felt them from his parents. But the question itself—"Do you like me?"—is a trap the therapist must avoid. There is too much social sham built into it, so much complicated fakery that a verbal assent is meaningless. Besides which, the real questions it masks are, *Am I human? Am I worth anything?*

In which case the therapist might silently say *no*—whereupon he must end the relationship as painlessly as posible. Or he might feel the *yes* deep within. One always feels the yes if yes it is. Yes makes it all easy; there is little, if any, sense of working in the relationship. A connection is made, the gratification missing in the parent-child relationship begins to generate, one retraces steps that were absent on the way to chronological maturity, and choices become apparent. Steps in human emotional development cannot be skipped with the coolness of promoting a bright child into a much higher grade. These steps must be experienced; if they have not been, a person must retreat into time and pluck them from the quicksand.

Yet for adults these "missed" childhood or adolescent experiences can never be regained in pure form; they can only be approximated. I have no doubt about this despite claims by such movements as Primal Therapy that now-buried feeling can be experienced exactly as it was during childhood. At best it is a "something-like" phenomenon; but "something like" is better than none at all. Picking up parental slack, the therapist must aid the patient to gratify himself—because only when the patient gratifies himself in the context of a human relationship do equality and growth coexist. The gratification that the therapist provides is simply the gratification of the relationship itself: an atmosphere of freedom, an atmosphere free of tyranny and interference.

But it is not idyllic or even simple. Far from it. Because people in any form of psychotherapy that stimulates insight and change take incredible chances. (Actually patients, at least for a time, feel that they are more reliant upon their therapists than they really are; but the feeling is necessary as a security device that fosters courage.) They risk losing the "truth" of their entrenched perceptions, the "truth" of their entire way of life. They are afraid of losing spouses and lovers, afraid of becoming homosexual, afraid of their rage and anxiety and depression, afraid that if they release their hold on what they have always believed to be reality, then they will lose all control and go mad. They are always aware that a way of life may be fake and ungratifying, but that there is also a security in what is known. The greatest sense of uneasiness for most people in psychotherapy stems from the possibility that there are all sorts of realities, that there is no one "truth," that life must be played essentially by ear, that anything can happen—and that when marked changes occur, one might not have the foggiest knowledge of the whys. For example, one of my patients has a quarrel with his wife but he cannot remember how they made up. He tries to grasp it intellectually but he can't. Finally, he shrugs his shoulders and says, "The only thing I can put my finger on is that we solved it just by living together."

It is something like a Zen process. Levels of awareness open, there is a sense of being able to do what you want, a greater feeling of living in the present, a release from the trap of time. Anxiety and depression are less troublesome because they come to be regarded as moods attached to living rather than symptoms that create panic. One begins to ride with the feelings instead of trying to combat them—combat making them "worse" and increasing the experience of helplessness. One begins to realize that it is acceptable to be either active *or* passive, that both are choices, that there is a time and place for either. It is not at all uncommon for a patient to express the feeling that he is involved in some sort of "Eastern" process, his feet on shifting sand; yet with a sense that all things are possible, that to be firmly rooted in the myth of reality is to be somehow catatonic, paralytic. Psychotherapy does not always lead to *satori*, but it can, at least to a limited extent; I qualify this because *satori* is almost impossible to translate into intellectual terms. D. T. Suzuki partly defines it

> as an intuitive looking into the nature of things in contradistinction to the analytical or logical understanding of it. . . . Or we may say that with satori our entire surroundings are viewed from quite an unexpected angle of perception.[2]

And a result of *satori* "is the revelation of a world of entirely new values."[3] One finally learns to trust intuition whereas before there was no faith in it whatever. Trust in intuition results from only one—but a profound—event: the acceptance of one's unconscious forces, "knowing" them even if the knowing is nonintellectual.

The more this intuitive, reflexive process develops, the less what is called psychotherapy is a "therapy." It becomes an absorption in the flow of life; the hour in the consultation room blends with other hours in the day. There are really no more "problems" because things are seen as what they are—which for Western man is probably the most powerful "unexpected angle of perception." There is less need to be burdened by the practicalities of living: you simply wash the dishes if they need washing; you don't question who left them for some insidious persecutory reason. (The struggle between husband and wife over who will do the laundry is a sublime absurdity.) And one is no longer emotionally afraid of others because the truth is revealed that there is nothing at all to fear. One merely lives; the world becomes myriad worlds.

This is no longer psychotherapy or psychoanalysis. It has nothing to do with such issues as the resolution of the Oedipus complex. It is total experience—yet one that requires another person as *all human life* requires other people. Even the student of Zen needs the Zen master, who ultimately is seen not as a master at all, but as a person who avoids systems and rules and who confuses his pupil whenever he perceives that the pupil *thinks* that he has found The Way. In the same way, as the good therapist helps his patient to dissolve defensive shams, the patient necessarily becomes confused, anxious, protests that he is "worse" or is going crazy. Because the world he has always known becomes not the only world that exists. And when this is accepted, a person *sees*. Somehow the therapist is no longer there; metaphorically, there is some question that he ever was.

I have been describing a tone, a feeling, the core of what is surrounded by many hours of talk, touch, psychodrama, whatever the technical apparatus might be. And, of course, I am talking of people who are capable of such an experience—and that includes anyone who, for example, is capable of reading this book.

Nevertheless, you will not meet too many of these people, because what we call psychotherapy usually ends prematurely.

The patient "feels better," is less anxious or depressed, relates "better," gets a raise in pay. These are all sound goals (though in truth they are by-products) but we generally stop just short of the finale—which is when a person confronts himself fully and admits to himself all that he really is. A leap into the abyss, the remainder of the unknown. Here, I think, is where traditional psychoanalysis fails miserably: it is simply too intellectualized. At best it constructs for the patient a superior set of defenses. One talks one's "problems" into a stupor of trivia: weary, the neurosis may hide, but it never leaves. Too beaten to be free, the patient adjusts.

I also want to give a sense of what I have been describing to the students I help train as therapists. When they ask me what makes a good therapist, I might quote Caruso's requisites for a good singer: "a big mouth, ninety percent memory, ten percent intelligence, lots of hard work and something in the heart." [4] Or I might tell them that I don't know; or say nothing at all; or suggest that they will find out when they have no sense of "work" when they see their patients. But what they *must* do is enter into the process. Because they are going to become parental substitutes for a time and they must not abuse the trust of their patients who will use the relationship to grow.

I feel very strongly about this: I would no longer, except under circumstances of incredible emergency, refer a person to a therapist who has not been in therapy himself. (Actually, this is the first question a person should ask of a prospective therapist.) Otherwise there is the greater danger, I could justly say the inevitability, that the therapist will act out his unconscious wishes through his patients—a situation I have witnessed a number of times in both professional and social settings. We can control this to some extent by requiring or urging beginning therapists to enter treatment; or if they balk, by simply scratching them from our referral lists. But we are powerless with parents; we can only suggest that they consider parenthood crucial enough to achieve some degree of readiness before they undertake what is perhaps the greatest of all responsibilities.

Of course, I am advocating a kind of broad therapeutic education for all parents, teachers, any parental substitutes. Insight into oneself must produce some in-touchness with the child's world. But I want to make one important point: an *intellectual* knowledge of the steps in a child's development, both emotional and cognitive, is not good enough. Recognizing this, a professor of education and child development at a prominent teacher's college years ago offered credit to any graduate students who entered psychotherapy.

This is needed because for centuries we have approached children with an emotional blindness. The past has mythologized the child on a continuum ranging from a wild beast in need of taming to a sexless confection—like the standard toy dolls which still do not have genitals. The truth is that children are people with a complexity of drives, wishes, and fantasies that are capable of persisting in pure form into adulthood. There is love inside them, and hate and murder and incest, and if we pretend otherwise, then we are denying those forces within ourselves.

I would love to see the following interchange: a little boy tells his mother that he has sexual feelings for her and she answers, "Of course you have. How else would you learn to love another woman?" In various forms—often even nonverbal—this sort of communication exists in a therapeutic relationship when a patient, working through his feelings of being possessed, of being a child, is ready to explore the possibilities of love and sex Out There.

As adults we generally see the primitive elements within us only when we experience nightmares—which *always*, without exception, reveal the incredible, frightening helplessness, the intense rage, that we lived through and felt as children. We see them, but often slough off the awareness as "only a dream." (In the same way we sledgehammer our way out of the pain of a depression instead of using it as a tool of insight; in a depression we are very close to ourselves.) But we cannot afford to slough it off. If we gain the courage to face where we are still stuck in childhood, we can let our children free themselves. But we appear to be continually intimidated by the idea of freedom—like the pipe smoker in William Steig's famous cartoon who, noticing a break in the chain that has been binding him, exclaims, "My God!"

Strangely enough, people have always bought psychologically oriented "how-to" books on child-raising. This is good, but it is still less than a halfway measure because there is no opportunity for dialogue with the authors. And without dialogue, telling points may be dismissed because they threaten us. We can merely close the book; it won't object. There is no one, as in a group setting, who can say, "Wait. Why are you tossing that idea away? Are *you* hung up there?" By reading we rarely permit ourselves to be emotionally touched by ideas and interpretations that may be true but abrasive—a sort of parallel to the classic failure of introspection as a means of self-therapy. Our brains "outthink" our capacity for emotional insight; we wind up simply rationalizing our feelings and behavior. We require another person to facilitate awareness of ourselves. Children, as well as we, are *human*—and it is that, the ingredients that make us human and not only animal, to which we must address our efforts and understanding.

We know so little about our children because we know so little about ourselves. The old psychoanalytic metaphor still holds: like an iceberg, seven-eighths of ourselves are invisible. But we, more human and resourceful than the iceberg, can bring more of ourselves to the surface. If we can set that tone now, communicate it to future generations, psychotherapists may one day be out of work. And *that* ought to be a goal.

Once I know myself as well as I can, then, if I wish, I can choose to be free. Then I will help free my children from the once "dark" wishes of my unconscious. They will go their own way—but I will always have them. Because unfettered by my fear and ignorance they will *want* to be my children.

Now there is one final question.

11

The Future
of Being Human

What of the distant future?

A question impossible to approach without some brief consideration of two very personal, very complex, ways of being—optimism and pessimism, and the almost infinite admixtures of both. They are intensely individual and varying character states because they depend upon and are formed by a great many mutually influential elements: how you were raised emotionally and ideologically; the positive, negative, and even neutral impact of environmental forces; what you know and understand; what you don't know and don't understand; and your degree of narcissism. Optimism and pessimism are essentially emotional views of the world, of destiny. The *amount* you express can be quantified and scaled by the use of rudimentary statistics, but they remain purely emotional concepts. Better put, they are the end products of all the forces working within us—which then we usually attempt to justify via intellectual explanations permeated by historical and scientific "data."

Pessimism is a time-honored position: today, as in past centuries, it is the reputable, accepted view of scientists, philosophers, and most brands of social thinkers. We must ask why this is so. Why do the undercurrents of doom flood to the surface in the final works of great innovators such as Schopenhauer, Freud, lately Konrad Lorenz? When all the intellectualizations are cleared away, predictions of the holocaust are embedded in bitter feelings of having been rejected by *all* of mankind, of having failed to bring the entire human race into the camp of one's unassailable "truth." This is a far cry from a clinical depression, a far cry from the despair of a black who is not permitted to live now. It is a vengeful reaction to a world that refuses to honor personal omnipotence. And so one ultimately says, "Go to hell. You will all kill yourselves and become extinct. But I could have saved you if only you had listened." Or as Lorenz comments, ". . . the author feels like a prophet crying in the wilderness . . . offended by the fact that no human being is listening to his crying. . . ." [1]

The statement hits dead center; and notice the messianic, religious language—the equation between the potential intellectual savior of the human race and the religio-spiritual savior of the human race. Obviously there is a raging arrogance in this view of the world, a narcissistic grandiosity that demands to be heard, loved, praised, adulated, worshiped. Of course the arrogance of these men always lay beneath the surface of their creative work, the spinning of their philosophies and psychologies. Only when the world does not act convinced that these are apotheoses does the vindictiveness and rage explode. Then the moneylenders in the temple must be whipped, driven out, and consigned to hell.

The pessimistic-narcissistic position supports itself with evidence of plagues, dinosaur extinction, pollution, food additives, Hiroshima, man's inhumanity to man. But its blind spot is abysmal, best illustrated by a central point of Milton's seventeenth-century theology: God cannot create a weight greater than he can lift. It is a point utterly applicable to the human being; indeed, on a broad evolutionary level, it may well be a definition of mankind. But pessimists *insist* that we (being superior to God) consistently create weights that must overwhelm us. Which is highly improbable. To flip the coin: the society is the great, inflexible, oppressive machine, supposedly more powerful than all of us. Yet we are caught on the horns of the irreducible fact that human beings create societies and perpetuate them because they need them; and when people need them to change functionally, they will change them. If we get ourselves into trouble, we will get ourselves out of it.

In essence, we cannot do more than we can do. We cannot think thoughts that exceed what we are capable of thinking. Nor can we dream dreams that cannot be dreamed.

The centuries-old arguments for universal catastrophe have always been remarkably similar. In the age of the plagues, cure seemed inconceivable; now we are supposed to perish from environmental pollution—another form of plague. The fears are essentially identical but the causes of disaster are, appropriately, specific to particular eras. More than that, they are specific to particular forms of ignorance. As medieval man could not dream of even the apparatus that would create the plagues of our century, we similarly cannot dream of a time when ecological messes will be controlled. Again, we cannot dream, at any point in evolutionary time, of what we cannot dream. But if we gain access to our inner wishes and fantasies, we will understand more about what we are really capable of dreaming; we will not be so terribly bound by what we *think* is reality.

I have said before that we have very little awareness of our struggle to be human and often do not know when we are being dehumanized. So, too, another crucial factor in the agonies of our evolution is that we generally don't know that we *are* evolving. I doubt that any species does. We can speculate about it, but it produces little impact. Except for a very few remarkable people, past and present, we have always considered ourselves the peak, the culmination of Homo sapiens—and this belief must necessarily play a dominant role in our love affair with doom. Because if we believe that we have leveled off, that we are *it*, then we fall victim to ideas of stagnation and decay. Where, then, is there left to go? It is difficult for us to understand, accept, or feel the slowness of our development. Even individually this feeling is impossibly elusive—unless we live in the now, and take chances, seek fresh experiences. Also, we can record historical data, find it repetitive (yet a thousand years is only a pinpoint of time), and use the observation to maintain that no further movement is probable. Besides which, recorded history is really a record of behavior, and we are only dimly aware of the reasons behind the behavior. As yet we are not fully capable of seeing, of catching, the internal movements; so far we can only grasp the obvious.

Over the past fifty years, anthropological and animal studies—particularly in the science of ethology—have shown us how close we still remain to our *nonhuman* ancestors. Nevertheless, we go on wanting to believe that we sit at the pinnacle: we have created biblical evidence to support this want, call it divine and hence unimpeachable truth, and continue to believe it. We have always created evidence to legitimize what we need to believe, then finally become trapped by it and relinquish it, but not without individual and social upheavals—and a strong sense of embarrassment.

Thus, as I see it, so much of what underlies historical behavior is the almost imperceptible paring away of those elements that are not necessary to our survival as a species—formalized religion being the most obvious example, since it is rooted in primitive needs and is now becoming anachronistic, vestigial.

In this context we can examine from a different angle the meaning or function of unconscious messages from parent to child. While at times they may be *personally* destructive, they produce change without the wrench of *social* destruction. The change is slow, while the structure stands, changing even more slowly. Man will not, cannot, cut roots abruptly; he must cling to some remnant of what he knows and can understand.

Examples of how tenaciously resistant we are to the idea that we are not a fixed or finished species are all about us, and there are countless things that we don't understand. Why, for example, are there billions of brain cells that don't seem to function? Or do they—in some way not observable by the present state of our science? We simply do not understand, or are awed into submission by, how unfinished we truly are. While we sacrifice so much of our personal freedom to the social structures we have created for stability and "meaning," consciously we are relatively unconcerned with our development as a species. I suspect that this absence of genuine concern has much to do with the fact that we die—that we as *individuals* have a circumscribed number of years. And no matter how we attempt to deal (or not deal) with this inevitability, that knowledge takes priority over any concern with species survival or development. (Ecologists and conservationists apparently have a greater sense of species, perhaps because they spend so much time close to nature; as opposed to such groups as construction workers who see in antipollution measures the potential loss of steady employment.)

Because I think, I think of my finiteness, the time boundaries of *my* life. I am not a termite that can reflexively, thoughtlessly, defend my colony against an ant attack in order to perpetuate collective development. My death is the death of the world—and that, too, is a component in prognoses of doom. Pessimism is a major way of dealing with the fear of death: I die and mankind dies with me and I don't want to acknowledge the possibility of brighter days that will dawn without me. Yet we move along, too; donating money to conquer disease, bearing children, doing countless things powerfully aimed at propagating the species and preserving it biologically. But our brain, our *conscious* thinking apparatus, must catch up with our silent and hidden sense of species. One day it will—because one day it will have to.

That will be part of our waking up, just as the current emphasis on awareness and emotional growth is part of individual awakening. The proliferation of various psychotherapies and awareness techniques is in no way artificial. Quite simply, we are ready for it. We are not just beginning: we are just beginning to be ready.

Perhaps the main undercurrent of this book has been to underline our resistance to the conscious knowledge that we are in subtle perpetual motion, repelling that knowledge while all the while urging movement and change through our children. With more awareness of our inner life, the urging can be more conscious and our "suffering" will decrease accordingly. The value of living now, on an individual level, sets us free because we *are* finite. The collective need for evolutionary development takes care of itself; yet we might enjoy that too if we really need to find a purpose in life. My purpose is simply to live as fully as possible; the purpose of my species is to *live on* in order to provide a context for living fully as a human being.

Our struggle to be human is more complex because we are more complex than other organisms. I can hear my neighbor bewailing his plight, while another neighbor experiences no plight whatever, while still another neighbor sympathizes with the justice of both positions. But when I see an old film—and there are many examples of this—of Frenchmen fleeing en masse from Paris in the face of Nazi attack, then I get a sense of collective necessity, and I see more clearly how we move as a species. As my children will see it in a more positive way when collective remedial measures are brought to bear on pollution and starvation. I can even soften my initial remark about moon travel: exploration of space might not only tell us more about our origins, it may well stimulate *feelings* about our origins.

So I do not think that we are going to eliminate or immolate ourselves. We will continue to struggle on in our individual and collective ways. We will become fully human—but not, as pessimists say, *despite* ourselves. We will become human *because* of ourselves,

Chapter Notes

CHAPTER 2

1. R. D. Laing, *The Self and Others*. London: Tavistock Publications, 1961.

CHAPTER 3

1. B. F. Skinner, *Beyond Freedom and Dignity*. New York: Knopf, 1971.
2. *Ibid.*

CHAPTER 4

1. Rollo May, *Love and Will*. New York: Norton, 1969.
2. Peter Blos, *On Adolescence*. New York: Free Press, 1962.

CHAPTER 5

1. Erving and Miriam Polster, *Gestalt Therapy Integrated*. New York: Brunner/Mazel, 1973.
2. Sigmund Freud, *Civilization and Its Discontents*. New York: Doubleday (Anchor Books), 1968.
3. Isshū Miura and Ruth Fuller Sasaki, *The Zen Koan*. New York: Harcourt, Brace and World, 1965.

4. Harry Stack Sullivan, *The Interpersonal Theory of Psychiatry*. New York: Norton, 1953.
5. D. W. Winnicott, *The Maturational Process and the Facilitating Environment*. New York: International Universities Press, 1966.

CHAPTER 7

1. Robert Briffault, *The Mothers*. New York: Grosset and Dunlap (Universal Library), 1963.
2. Ernest Jones, *The Life and Work of Sigmund Freud* (Vol. I). New York: Basic Books, 1953.

CHAPTER 9

1. "Sexual Deviations. Homosexuality," in *Diagnostic and Statistical Manual of Mental Disorders*. Washington: American Psychiatric Association, 1968.
2. Lionel Ovesey, *Homosexuality and Pseudohomosexuality*. New York: Science House, 1969.

CHAPTER 10

1. Irvin D. Yalom, *The Theory and Practice of Group Psychotherapy*. New York: Basic Books, 1970.
2. D. T. Suzuki, *Essays in Zen Buddhism* (First Series). New York: Grove Press (Evergreen), 1961.
3. *Ibid.*
4. Dorothy Caruso, *Enrico Caruso, His Life and Death*. New York: Simon and Schuster, 1945.

CHAPTER 11

1. Konrad Lorenz, *Civilized Man's Eight Deadly Sins*. New York: Harcourt Brace Jovanovich, 1974.